Working with Children and Adolescents in Residential Care

Working with Children and Adolescents in Residential Care: A Strengths-Based Approach is written for professionals who work with children and youth in out of home placements, be they social services workers, child welfare or family court workers, educators, or mental health professionals in general. The book offers an approach that these professionals can use to positively impact the lives of young people in residential facilities. The book emphasizes the strengths and abilities of young people from the assessment phase of treatment through discharge, and helps readers to take into account the views and actions of youth in order to provide clients appropriate services. This new volume includes sections on principles of effective youth care work, personal philosophy, positive youth development, teamwork, staffings, and crisis management.

Bob Bertolino, PhD, is an Associate Professor of Rehabilitation Counseling at Maryville University, Missouri, USA, and Senior Clinical Advisor at Youth In Need, Inc. He is also a Senior Associate for the International Center for Clinical Excellence (ICCE), and he maintains a private practice and provides consultation and training.

Working with Children and Adolescents in Residential Care
A Strengths-Based Approach

Bob Bertolino

NEW YORK AND LONDON

First published 2015
by Routledge
711 Third Avenue, New York, NY 10017

and by Routledge
27 Church Road, Hove, East Sussex BN3 2FA

Routledge is an imprint of the Taylor & Francis Group,
an informa business

© 2015 Taylor & Francis

The right of Bob Bertolino to be identified as author of this work has been asserted by him in accordance with sections 77 and 78 of the Copyright, Designs and Patents Act 1988.

All rights reserved. No part of this book may be reprinted or reproduced or utilized in any form or by any electronic, mechanical, or other means, now known or hereafter invented, including photocopying and recording, or in any information storage or retrieval system, without permission in writing from the publishers.

Trademark notice: Product or corporate names may be trademarks or registered trademarks, and are used only for identification and explanation without intent to infringe.

Library of Congress Cataloging-in-Publication Data
Bertolino, Bob, 1965–
  Working with children and adolescents in residential care : a strengths-based approach / by Bob Bertolino.
    pages cm
  Includes bibliographical references and index.
  1. Youth—Institutional care. 2. Youth—Services for. 3. Group homes for children. 4. Group homes for youth. 5. Social work with children, 6. Social work with youth. 7. Child care workers. I. Title.
  HV862.B47 2015
  362.73'2—dc23
  2014039310

ISBN: 978-1-138-85615-8 (hbk)
ISBN: 978-1-138-85613-4 (pbk)
ISBN: 978-1-315-71987-0 (ebk)

Typeset in Sabon
by Apex CoVantage, LLC

To youth care workers around the world: My deepest gratitude for your contributions to the lives of youth—past, present, and future. Your efforts strengthen and change lives every day.

Contents

Preface	ix
Acknowledgments	xi

1 A Day in the Life: The Many Faces of Residential
   Youth Care Workers   1

2 Something to Believe In: Orienting Toward Possibilities   21

3 Making Contact: Creating a Respectful Climate   36

4 We're in This Together: Teaming Up for Change   67

5 There's More Than One Way: Strategies for Change   92

6 In the Moment: Strategies for Crisis Prevention   124

7 The Circle of Lives: Future Roads of Possibility   144

References	167
Index	173

Preface

I began my career as a residential youth care worker (RYCW) in the late 1980s. I was fortunate to learn from an extraordinary group of people. I made mistakes, got up, made more mistakes, and got up again. I doubted myself time after time. Any job that is as simultaneously challenging and rewarding as that of a RYCW is, as they say, worth doing. And although I am no longer a RYCW, I still work in youth and family services (YFS) and with RYCWs every day. This book is for anyone and everyone who gives completely of themselves to better the lives of youth.

How This Book Is Arranged

Working with Children and Adolescents in Residential Care is divided into seven chapters.

The first chapter is "A Day in the Life: The Many Faces of Residential Youth Care Workers." This chapter explores three distinct areas. The first is the roles and responsibilities of RYCWs. We learn the multifaceted role of RYCWs and how they truly are the heart and soul of residential services. Second, we learn about the role of RYCWs' personal philosophies, which are a determining factor in the effectiveness of services. The third distinct area of Chapter 1 is an introduction to the *collaborative, strengths-based approach*, which becomes the basis for the book.

Chapter 2 is "Something to Believe In: Orienting Toward Possibilities." In this chapter we focus on the difference between traditional pathology and deficit conversations and collaborative, strengths-based conversations. In addition, this chapter explores the role of personal philosophy—how RYCWs see youth and change and envision residential services as a whole.

"Making Contact: Creating a Respectful Climate" is the third chapter. Here we focus on initial contacts—in particular, initial information-gathering processes. A core aspect of this chapter also involves core attending and listening skills, which every RYCW should be familiar with and practice.

Chapter 4, "We're in This Together: Teaming Up for Change," emphasizes the role of teams in residential settings. A specific area of discussion is staffings and team meetings. Also included in this chapter are x *Preface*

suggestions for shift changes and coping with frustration that can build over the course of shift work.

"There's More Than One Way: Strategies for Change" is Chapter 5. This entire chapter is dedicated to a variety of strategies that can be used by RYCWs to facilitate change with youth. Included in this chapter are methods for changing views and actions, as well as how to create a foundation for change that is based on Positive Youth Development (PYD).

Next is "In the Moment: Strategies for Crisis Prevention." This chapter includes prevention ideas and intervention strategies. In particular, emphasis is on de-escalation of youth. A further area of focus in Chapter 6 is on-call systems.

Chapter 7, "The Circle of Lives: Future Roads of Possibility," is the final chapter. The book comes to a close with a discussion about how to work with youth when they are not progressing, deteriorating, or improving. A key point in this chapter is the creation of a responsive climate. In addition, ideas for how to amplify change, prepare youth for future challenges, and transition from services are offered.

The Language

In each of my books, I address the issue of language, which is a tricky proposition when it comes to not only residential services but YFS as a whole. Because terms will vary from program to program, RYCWs will be required to adapt to the syntax of their settings. For the purposes of this book, a variety of terms will be used, all of which are meant to be respectful of youth, supportive others, RYCWs, and those involved with YFS in general.

For starters, the term "strengths" will be used primarily and is synonymous with "competence" or "competency." At their core, these terms connote a focus on abilities, resources, and change. In addition, the term "youth" will be used in reference to ages 8 through 21. Although I've chosen to emphasize this age range, the ideas described throughout have been and can be easily adapted to services offered to younger children and older adults. I will also periodically use terms including, but not limited to, "counseling," "therapy," "prevention," "education," "investigation," "case management," "social services," and so on. These descriptors are meant to highlight specific types of services. I will also use terms such as "interactions," "meetings," "sessions," "appointments," and "intakes" interchangeably. Although the terminology may need to be adjusted, it is the ideas that are paramount.

Bob Bertolino
September 2014

Acknowledgments

Thank you to Misha, Morgan, Claire and my entire family for your love, support, and understanding. I love you. To the staff of Youth In Need (YIN), Inc. for creating space for me to grow, learn, and try out new ideas. We are defined by our relationships, and for over 20 years YIN has connected me to many extraordinary people. A special thank you to Pat Holterman-Hommes, Tricia Topalbegovic, Michelle Gorman, Mark Solari, Rob Muschany, April Delehaunty, Amy Putzler, Keri Young, Amy Brown, Melanie Rodman, Chris Turner, Cara Merritt, Erin Strohbehn, Rachel Woepke, Andre Young, Dawn Hiatt, Kendan Elliott, Stephanie Williams, Brittanie Gellings, and YIN staff of past and present. To my colleagues at Maryville University: Michael Kiener, Kate Kline, Mya Vaughn, Dean Chuck Gulas, and former and present students, thank you for your support. To my friends and colleagues: Bill O'Hanlon, Scott Miller, Charlie Appelstein, Calvin Smith, Adrian Blow, Susanne Bargmann, Jason Seidel, Rob Axsen, and Cynthia Maeschalck, and the International Center for Clinical Excellence (ICCE), you continue to shape my life immeasurably. And I would like to extend my heartfelt appreciation to Routledge/Taylor & Francis family. Especially, George Zimmar, for seeing the value in my ideas.

1 A Day in the Life
The Many Faces of Residential Youth Care Workers

What first interested you in the field of Youth and Family Services (YFS)? What about residential care, specifically? I have over the years heard many intriguing stories about how people became affiliated with YFS. I too have a story, one that begins with a job as a resident counselor in an emergency shelter for displaced, troubled, and homeless youth. It's a job that I almost did not get.

In 1989 I spotted an ad for employment at an agency by the name of Youth In Need. Not only did I have any idea what a resident counselor was, but the only thing I knew about Youth In Need was that it was a nonprofit—at least that's what the ad said. I knew about nonprofits since I was working on an undergraduate degree in social work. I also played nightclubs in bands that barely made enough to survive—which, by my definition, made us nonprofits.

I applied and to my surprise was offered an interview. It was on a Monday at the agency's emergency shelter, which aside from signage out front with the name "Youth In Need" looked like the other houses around it. I was as unprepared as one could be. I wondered: *What do they do here? What might I be asked to do if hired? What if I blow it?* The longer I waited, the more unanswerable questions populated my imagination.

As I sat nervously in the foyer, I heard a sound that was out of context. It was a guitar. Not from a song on a nearby radio, but rather from a guitar being played somewhere in the "house." The sound was faint, leading me to think I was hearing things. But there was a distinguishing characteristic of the sound that let me know it was quite real—the guitar was *very out of tune.*

Being a marginal musician didn't get in the way of my living and breathing music. No matter how out of tune the guitar, I had to find the source. In a music-induced trance, I followed the warbly twang down a narrow hallway, arriving at a set of double doors. Peering in, I saw what resembled a family room—a hangout of sorts—a place to chat, read, maybe watch TV. The room was plain, with flat white walls and a few sparse furnishings. The decorations resembled those of just about any physician's office waiting room.

2 A Day in the Life

What made the room unique was the source of the "music"—a young man with a glossy red Fender Stratocaster knockoff. The youth sat on a couch, fully immersed in playing his unplugged electric guitar. Dressed in jeans and a long black overcoat—not unlike the one I had on—he strummed away before noticing me and rising from the couch. Because I had not thought things out, I was startled when the youth spotted me. I briefly considered running for the door but offered instead to tune his guitar. His response was an exuberant yes.

I soon learned that his name was Adam and that he was 15 years old. It was clear from the get-go that music was a big part of Adam's life. I knew little more than his name before he began listing his favorite bands and songs. He seemed to have an encyclopedic knowledge of current music. While Adam's voice conveyed his excitement about music, it was his eyes that revealed his passion.

The conversation unfolded quickly. Adam told me he was away from home because of problems with his dad. The more he spoke the more I began to understand what brought kids to Youth In Need. Although my perception of the agency was just starting to evolve, it was clear to me that youth like Adam were experiencing dire circumstances. I was transfixed by what Adam had to say. I may have been drawn to the room by the sound of his guitar, but it was his story and the melodies that made up his life that enveloped me.

It was a matter of time before Adam got around to asking questions of me. It turned out he only had one. He asked, "What is your job here?" Just as I was about to tell him I was there for an interview, a woman entered the room. "There you are!" she yelped. The woman was the shelter director, Laura. She had gone to the front foyer to get me for the interview only to find me playing guitar with Adam. I was embarrassed but tried to remain calm as I wished Adam well and headed with Laura to the interview.

My questions about Youth In Need, which I learned was called "YIN," were answered during the interview. I learned that the building we were in, "The Shelter," was the focal point of the agency, started as an alternative for displaced children and youth. The pieces of the puzzle came together quickly, and it all made sense.

I made it through the interview, relying mostly on what I had gleaned from school and, well, life experience. As I left Youth In Need, I walked down the same hallway that had led me to Adam. I wondered what would become of him.

Over the next few days, I thought about the entire experience at Youth In Need again and again. I realized I shouldn't have wandered down the hallway and gone into the room where Adam was. I wasn't an employee. I didn't have permission. But at the time, those thoughts had not crossed my mind. What I saw was Adam the person—not Adam who was in a home for kids. Naïve as it may be, I saw him no differently than someone I would encounter on the street. I met a person who like me enjoyed music, someone I could do something nice for, like tune his guitar. I had to leave it at that.

I got the job.

Sometime later, Laura told me why I had been hired as a resident counselor. It wasn't because of how I answered the interview questions—which was unremarkable—or my level of professional experience—which was zero—or anything seemingly relevant to the interview. It was because of what she witnessed in those brief moments between Adam and me. She saw something in me that let her know I would be a good choice for the job and was worth taking a chance on. What others might have considered drawbacks to hiring me, Laura saw as strengths.

It has been more than 20 years since that interview. I have had many different positions at Youth In Need, and while I also hold a university faculty position, I still work at the same agency. What about you? What's your story? I invite you to take a moment to reflect on the following questions:

- What compelled me to start working in YFS?
- What do I *now* find most compelling about YFS?
- How do I cope with the uncertainties that accompany my role?
- What do I do to embrace the role of youth care worker (YCW), including the ups and downs?
- How do I face the daily challenges of being a YCW?
- What do I do or tell myself when things don't go as planned? [e.g., with a particular youth, on a shift or interaction, etc.]
- What do I need to be a successful YCW?
- What keeps me in YFS (and as a YCW)?
- How can I have the greatest impact in my role?
- How can my work be even more meaningful?
- What can I do to continue to challenge myself and improve my skills over the course of my career?

Beyond what initially drew you to YFS, what keeps you there? And if you work in a residential program, what is it about your everyday work that fuels your passion? It can be helpful to revisit these questions from time to time. You are encouraged to also consider what you already do to meet the challenges of being a RYCW and what you will need in the future to grow as your career evolves. You are important, and we need you. This book is for you.

Here, There, and Everywhere: Profiling the Residential Youth Care Worker

As described in the preface, youth in out-of-home placements, be they short- or long-term, are served in a variety of settings, including emergency and runaway shelters, residential treatment and group home facilities,

4 A Day in the Life

inpatient psychiatric units, intensive outpatient and partial day treatment options (e.g., substance abuse or eating disorder clinics), juvenile and other corrections facilities, and independent and transitional living programs. Typically, residential programs house anywhere from a handful (such as emergency or crisis care shelters when census is low) to several dozen youth (as with large state-run institutions). Residential facilities vary in terms of youth served including age ranges, gender, length of stay, and, in some cases, demographic areas served. For example, some will only take youth in the custody of the state while others will also accept private placements. In addition, out-of-home placements can be very generalized or specific in terms of the type of services offered. Programs may focus exclusively on substance abuse rehabilitation or youth who have histories of violent behavior, for example.

A common thread in each of the settings listed are residential youth care workers. Depending on the program, RYCWs are sometimes referred to as resident or youth counselors, psychiatric technicians (psych techs), child or youth care workers, or house parents or managers. RYCWs are not only necessary to the everyday operations of residential facilities, they are arguably *the* most important form of personnel. It's very simple: Without RYCWs there would not be residential programs.

It was once believed that the "important" therapeutic work in residential facilities was provided by clinical staff composed of counselors, social workers, psychologists, psychiatrists, and the like. And although teams are responsible for care in residential programs, at the center of teams are RYCWs. It is RYCWs who spend the most time with youth and, ultimately, have more opportunities than any other professional to positively influence their lives. Although the responsibilities and duties of RYCWs may vary from facility to facility and program to program, there are common elements that run through all of these positions. General duties of RYCWs include the following:

- Providing safety, physical care, supervision, discipline, emotional connection, and educational support to youth (program ratios of staff to youth can vary according to licensing and funding requirements; for example, some program will maintain a ratio of one staff member per six youth);
- Completing and/or overseeing daily program tasks and functions;
- Conducting face-to-face or telephonic screenings and/or intake interviews (assessments);
- Meeting formally or informally with youth;
- Leading educational, support, and/or treatment groups;
- Managing crises with youth and in programs;
- Participating in the physical upkeep of facilities; and,
- Working as part of a team that may include other mental health and social service workers, health professionals, educators, and recreational specialists (Bertolino, 2014).

The responsibilities of RYCWs do not end with formal job descriptions. Instead, most RYCWs are familiar with the phrase, "Other duties as assigned." RYCWs are in effect the "go-to" persons—preserving the safety and well-being of youth while juggling multiple on-shift tasks. On a given shift a RYCW could be supervising several "residents," working to resolve a conflict between two youth, and monitoring a crisis call line, with documentation awaiting. RYCWs not only have numerous responsibilities, but they carry out those responsibilities in environments that are fast-paced and require conscientious, on-the-spot decision making.

Like nurses or emergency room residents in training, RYCWs accept that shifts may long and include overnights. Some overnights are "sleep shifts" in which a staff member sleeps but may be awakened if a crisis arises. A benefit of residential programs is that RYCWs can often arrange to work shifts that accommodate school or other work schedules.

The are many dualities involved with the role of the RYCW, the most fundamental of which is serving both in a therapeutic capacity and a position of authority. In one moment a RYCW might help calm a youth with suicidal thoughts who is having a panic attack. Later in the shift, the same staff person might give the consequence of a level drop to the very youth who was panicking earlier in the day. Over time RYCWs learn to negotiate such dualities day to day, shift by shift, and interaction by interaction. The RYCW is everything to everyone when it comes to out-of-home placement.

But there is another, much more pervasive duality that lingers within the psyche of the RYCW that can, at minimum, whittle away at the faith of RYCWs and, if left unchecked, spell the end of careers. RYCWs, like many in mental health and social services, choose to help the most vulnerable. Study after study supports the need of prevention and intervention services to children, youth, and families. These studies are backed by public sentiment that largely reflects a societal value placed on caring for those who are unable to care for themselves. Herein is the duality for the RYCW. Despite the value placed on caring for our young, the first funding cuts are often made are to mental health and social services. And as the saying goes, "No money, no mission." Even the most committed RYCW experiences disappointment arising from the hypocrisy of providing services that society states it values but, in the end, does not want to fund. That equation proves to be too much for many.

Other threats to longevity of RYCWs include long hours, unrelenting job responsibilities, and low salaries. Without awareness, guidance, and support, the role of the RYCW can seem too much. Let's add it up. First is the emotional distress on providers who are doing the work in the name of helping others. Next is the effect of staff turnover on the quality of care to youth. The pool of qualified individuals willing to work for high stress and low pay has dwindled substantially over the past two decades. RYCW positions used to be appealing to persons who had just completed their bachelor's degree and/or were perhaps pursuing a master's. Not any

6   A Day in the Life

longer. When fast food restaurants pay more than the average agency residential program, there is a problem.

The impact? Turnover rates with frontline staff, particularly those in residential setting, average between 22%–60% annually, with some agencies having as much as 75% of their staff with less than 1 year of experience (Barford & Whelton, 2010; Hwang & Hopkins, 2012; Proyouthwork America, 2011; Wilson, 2009). To hire and train each new staff member costs between $7,000 to $12,000. So if you are a RYCW and are beyond 1 year of service, you have surpassed the odds of attrition. And if your organization has an annual turnover rate among frontline staff at or below 20%, you are accomplishing something extraordinary.

Now for the good news. There are many who understand and support quality mental health and social services for youth and families. In addition, please know how valuable you and your efforts are. There is nothing more important than giving of ourselves. The first purpose of this book is to help you stay connected with what inspired you to go into YFS to being with. Inspiration is both healing and contagious. The second purpose is to provide ways of building on the knowledge and ability you already possess so that your work can be even more beneficial to youth and families.

The Long and Winding Road: An Evolving Perspective for Residential Youth Care Workers

History reveals that most residential programs were founded on principles associated with the medical model—focusing on deficit and pathology. The prevailing theory was that at minimum there was something wrong with youth (e.g., they were unable, incapable, or unwilling to change their behavior and/or cope; they could not overcome debilitating family problems or traumas; they lacked skills, etc.) and, at worst, youth were in some way "damaged." Michael Durrant (1993) stated, "Much residential work has reflected these ideas of children being damaged or disturbed, children processing some problem or pathology, or parents being incompetent or deficient" (p. 12). According to this perspective, the core questions has been, "What's wrong with youth?" The implications of such a question are far reaching. Durrant continues:

> If we approach our task from this viewpoint, inevitably we will see our role as that of experts who operate upon clients in order to fix or cure something. This view may be reflected in providing therapeutic care to help children "get over" damaging experiences, exerting control to modify unacceptable behavior and allow control to be internalized, prescribing tasks to alter dysfunctional family structure or processes, and so on.
>
> (p. 12)

Due to the long-standing influence of the deficit/pathology-based model, RYCWs have unknowingly found themselves in a difficult predicament. They have in effect become prisoners of systems that succeed in bringing out the worst rather than the best of youth. It is unfortunate that capable RYCWs have been trained in ways that too often impart the message that residential care is but a "holding tank" for youth before they move on to unfulfilling lives. And that very same message has then been passed along to youth and their support systems.

In my first year as a RYCW, I met a 12-year-old, Jeff, who had been brought to our emergency shelter for a family timeout. At the intake assessment, his mom stated, "Jeff's been in two other places and blew it both times. He acted like a fool—throwing things and cussing. They told me he was headed for jail. They said I shouldn't let him come home because he's a sociopath and won't change."

Now let's consider the good news. There is evidence that the foundational ideas and practices of residential care and YFS in general are evolving and taking root (Bertolino, 2011, 2014). Although it has been a gradual transition to move away from a pathology-oriented framework, it is happening. We are collectively gravitating toward the question, "What is right with youth?" This question points the compass of YFS toward strengths and possibilities. And holding that compass is the RYCW.

Where Do You Stand?
RYCWs and Philosophy

No matter the foundational approach of an organization or program in YFS—traditional/deficit driven or strengths based—each RYCW must decide where he or she "stands." We'll refer to our perspectives or worldviews as *personal philosophies* (Bertolino, 2014). Research makes it clear that the person of the RYCW (and any service provider in contact with youth) has a far greater influence on the benefit and eventual outcome of services than any technique or method employed (Brown, Lambert, Jones, & Minami, 2005; Luborsky et al., 1986; Wampold & Brown, 2005). Training is not enough to improve the effectiveness of a RYCW. Because YFS are reliant on human relationships, one's personal philosophy can substantially influence where a particular framework or orientation succeeds or fails.

The following questions can help RYCWs to better identify the beliefs and assumptions that form their personal philosophy:

- What are my core beliefs, ideas, or assumptions about youth (and families)?
- How have I come to believe what I believe about youth (and families)?
- What has most significantly influenced my beliefs, ideas, and assumptions as they relate to youth and families?

8 A Day in the Life

- How have my beliefs, ideas, and assumptions affected my work in YFS (and in residential settings, in particular)? With colleagues/peers? With the community at large?
- How do I believe that change occurs? What does change involve?
- Do I believe that some degree of change is possible with every youth? Every family (if applicable)? [If you answered yes, end here. If you answered no, proceed to the next question.]
- How do I work with youth (and families) whom I believe cannot (or do not want to or are resistant to) change? What do I do?
- If I do not believe that every youth (and/or family) can experience some degree of change, what keeps me in YFS? (Bertolino, 2014)

Personal philosophies are reflections of our attitudes. As such, personal philosophies are revealed through questions, techniques, and the like. Surgeon Atul Gawande (2007), the author of *Better: A Surgeon's Notes on Performance*, has said that the worst thing a physician can do is give up hope on a patient. The same can be said for those who work in mental health and social services. While most of my commentary involves suggestions and recommendations, I stand firm on one thing: It is imperative that RYCWs hold the belief that youth can change, grow, and have a promising future. This does not mean every youth has the ability to solve every problem. It does not mean downplaying physical and intellectual propensities. We do not trivialize or ignore the harsh realities that youth and those associated with youth face. Rather, we acknowledge those challenges while simultaneously seeing youth as having many capacities and resources that serve as building blocks to present and future change. Effective YCWs believe not only in the abilities of others, but they maintain a relentless pursuit of client strengths and employ those strengths to create future possibilities.

If you have mixed feelings on the idea of focusing on deficits versus strengths, you're not alone. What is critical is a willingness to reexamine your views. And if you are willing, the possibilities are endless for you and those with whom you work. Let's return to the story of Jeff, the 12-year-old I encountered early in my career as a RYCW:

> Jeff stayed in our emergency shelter program for two weeks. He then returned home, attending several aftercare sessions with the therapist who had been assigned to work with him and his mother. As with many youth who came through our program, we hoped for the best with Jeff but lost contact when the aftercare sessions ended.
>
> Two years later Jeff resurfaced. There had been a loss of a family member with whom Jeff was close, and his mother was concerned that he had not talked to anyone about it. When asked how things had been over the past years, Jeff's mother replied, "I don't think it's been any different than with most families. I don't know what the big

fuss was before." Jeff had in fact thrived in school and as a 14-year-old had made the honor role for the first time.

Although this particular youth was labeled as a "sociopath" by other mental health professionals, some of whom were RYCWs, he did not live out his life by this story. He coauthored a new life story with family, friends, and the staff members at the third and final facility at which he stayed. Jeff's change was not a fluke or the result of fortunate coincidences. This sort of change happens each and every day in our residential programs.

A Strengths-Based Perspective

Youth in residential placements come from difficult backgrounds. Many will have significant emotional, biological, cultural, social, psychological, interpersonal, and physical challenges. To help youth cope with these challenges effectively, we create safe contexts, the foundation of which is positive relationships. The success of residential services depends largely on the quality of relationships formed with youth. In fact, research has demonstrated that youth who are more engaged and involved in therapeutic processes are likely to receive greater benefit than those who are not (Orlinsky, Rønnestad, & Willutzki, 2004).

A benefit of the relationships formed with youth is that youth can take with them a sense of connection to others. When they fall down, as well as in times of self-doubt and worry, youth can remember those who stand in support. Knowing that others care can encourage youth to stay the course, remain resilient, and focus on the future.

> After I had become a therapist in our emergency shelter, the crisis hotline rang as I was standing in the staff office. Because we were an "all hands on deck" program and I was nearest to the phone, I took the call. I began with my usual introduction, "Youth In Need, this is Bob, can I help you?" "You already have," the person replied. I was confused and momentarily speechless. My initial hesitance was because we had had our share of prank calls—my favorite being when people would call to order Chinese food. Since the shelter was listed as "YIN House" in the phone book, we received calls from those who were pranking us and those who genuinely thought we were a Chinese restaurant. On this occasion I was quick to think it was the former.
>
> After a brief pause, I said, "I'm sorry, could you please say that again? I think I misunderstood." "You already have helped me," the caller reiterated. "Don't you remember me?" *Now I was mystified.* I inquired, "Were you calling for someone in particular?" The caller laughed, "Yes, I am calling for you! It's Kyle! Don't you remember me?" I scanned the Rolodex in my brain, and then it came to me. I knew several Kyles, but the caller could only be *that Kyle.*

10 *A Day in the Life*

I was quickly consumed with joy. Although I did not know why Kyle was calling, I did know that it had been a while since he had been with us. Because the youth we serve are often transient, we sometimes lose contact. We follow up but unfortunately there are those we never hear from again. So when we do reconnect, it is cause for celebration.

Kyle, now 21 (he was 17 when he was in the shelter), was living in another state training to be a police officer. He was pursuing the future in law enforcement he had described years earlier and was engaged to be married. After we talked for nearly 45 minutes, Kyle lowered his voice and said, "You know, I remember when my dad refused to let me come home and you talked with me. I just wanted to thank you."

After hanging up with Kyle, I thought about his days at the emergency shelter. I remembered many things, but not the conversation we had after his father refused to let him return home. Kyle was with us for nearly 3 months during a summer, and yet it was that one moment among many others that seemed to make the most difference for him.

Effective RYCWs have a variety of methods, techniques, and interventions from which to draw. And yet, the most underrated "tool" RYCWs have is themselves. When I talk with residential staff, I frequently hear stories similar to that of Kyle—single moments that made a substantial difference in the lives of youth. The attention of a single, caring RYCW or other staff person can and often does represent a starting point for youth to rewrite the stories of their lives. Now imagine what is possible when all residential staff work together in a unified direction.

A starting point for unification among residential staff begins with our personal philosophies. What follows is the philosophy of the organization and program. As discussed earlier in this chapter, residential programs have a long tradition of focusing on pathology. Here we explore a necessary alternative: a *strengths-based* approach. But what exactly does it mean to be strengths based? Here's a formal definition:

A strengths-based perspective emphasizes the abilities and resources people have within themselves and their support systems to more effectively cope with life challenges. When combined with new experiences, understandings and skills, these abilities and resources contribute to improved well-being, which is comprised of three areas of functioning: individual, interpersonal relationships, and social role. Strengths-based practitioners value relationships and convey this through respectful, culturally-sensitive, collaborative practices that support, encourage and empower. Routine and ongoing real-time feedback is used to maintain a responsive, consumer-driven climate to ensure the greatest benefit of services.

(Bertolino, 2014)

Notice that there are several parts to this definition. First is a focus on strengths and resources. Our aim is to identify and activate the already existing abilities and resources of youth. We also assist youth with expanding their perspectives and in developing new skills and systems of support. A strengths-based perspective is therefore two pronged, involving both the activation and utilization of latent or underemployed abilities and the teaching of new ones (Bertolino, 2014).

A second part of the strengths-based definition is the construct *well-being*. A construct is an idea to which different elements contribute. For example, weather is made up of temperature, barometric pressure, humidity, and the like. Each element is important but does not in and of itself define weather. Similarly, well-being is inclusive of three elements or areas: individual, interpersonal, and social role functioning. Individual functioning includes positive emotion, engagement, meaning, and accomplishment (Seligman, 2011). In brief, positive emotion includes but is not limited to happiness and life satisfaction. Engagement relates to subjective absorption through experiences in the present. Meaning equates to belonging to and serving something that is believed to be bigger than one's self. Accomplishment or achievement is the pursuit of something for its own sake and is commonly seen in the pursuit of success, competence, or mastery.

Another element of well-being is interpersonal functioning, which refers to close, often intimate, positive interactions with others. Most frequently this includes caregivers, family, and those who play significant roles in the lives of youth. The third and final area is social role functioning, an element that captures the impact of school, employment, community support, and other more general yet important forms of support. As with the elements of weather, each of the three areas of functioning is crucial but does not by itself define well-being; it is their collective value that forms well-being. Our aim for youth is to have greater degrees of well-being at the end of services.

The definition of strengths based includes a third component—a focus on relationships. Most important here is the supportive role that RYCWs play in the lives of youth. RYCWs view each interaction as an opportunity to work together toward a hoped-for future. To this end, strategies used to strengthen the alliance and promote change are provided with respect to the culture of the youth. The therapeutic alliance, which will be discussed later in this chapter, is arguably the most robust finding in psychotherapy literature.

The final part of the strengths-based definition is the role of routine and ongoing real-time feedback in evaluating the impact and benefit of services. Real-time feedback is composed of two forms of measurement: outcome and alliance. Outcome refers to the impact of services, from the client's perspective, on major areas of functioning: individual, interpersonal, and social role. Alliance or process measurement involves

12   *A Day in the Life*

elicitation of the client's perceptions of the therapeutic relationship. Routine (i.e., each session or meeting) and ongoing (i.e., from the start of services to discontinuation) feedback improves the effectiveness of services by allowing the client and his or her experiences to serve as a guide. For youth, a feedback focus creates a context in which their voices are not only expressed, but are heard and responded to.

Principles of a Strengths-Based Perspective

In previous publications I described assumptions or principles that characterize a collaborative, strengths-based (competency) perspective both in general practice (see Bertolino, 2010) and specific to youth care work (see Bertolino, 2014). These principles have evolved over time as research has matured and taught us more about successful practice. In their current form, the principles represent decades of empirical research. The purpose of the five strengths-based principles that follow is to provide guidance not only for RYCWs but for all who work in YFS.

The principles will be detailed through a three-level structure. The first level is a description of the principle itself. Next is the "primary competency" associated with the principle. The primary competency represents the overall skill for RYCWs to master. The third level includes 10 key tasks associated with the primary competency. For readers interested in additional tasks beyond those specific to RYCWs, the book *Thriving on the Front Lines: A Guide to Strengths-Based Youth Care Work* (Bertolino, 2014) offers an expanded overview.

There are two further points before we delve into the principles. First, the principles are interrelated. That is, each principle overlaps with, influences, and is influenced by the others. So as we consider how to employ a particular function, we simultaneously remain open to ways that the other four principles come into play. Second, principles serve only as guides. How the principles are utilized will depend on a RYCW's style and the fit with each individual youth. Abraham Maslow famously said, "If the only tool you have is a hammer, you'll treat the whole world like a nail." Ideas void of context are simply ideas. How you apply the principles is up to you.

Principle 1: Youth Are the Most Significant Contributors to Service Success

Primary Competency: Maximize Youth Contributions to Change

Referred to as "client factors" in the research, youth contribute between 80%–87% to the variance in outcome (Wampold, 2001). Client factors are largely represented through internal strengths and external resources. Internal strengths include optimism, persistence, resilience, protective

A Day in the Life   13

factors, coping skills, and abilities utilized in vocational, educational, and social settings. Resilience and protective factors are qualities and actions that allow youth to meet the difficulties and challenges of life. Growth and maturation relate to the ability of youth to move through or mature out of individual and life cycle developmental phases, manage the trials and tribulations of life, overcome problems, and cope with trauma (Bertolino, 2014). Resilience, protective factors, growth, and maturation are closely tied to one another. External resources refer to relationships, social networks, and systems that provide support and opportunities. Examples are family, friends, employment, and educational, community, and religious supports. External resources also include affiliation or membership in groups or associations that provide connection and stability. Youth support systems are central in maintaining long-term change; focusing on processes that tap into, develop, and encourage such capacities is central to a strengths-based perspective.

Client contributions also include opportunities for new learning and skill development. Psychoeducational and experiential activities are used to help youth develop a more encompassing repertoire of skills. A combination of already existing strengths and the addition of new skills is a formidable duo that provides youth with a broader range of options and responses for coping with life challenges. To make the most of the contributions of youth, it is necessary that YCWs become versed in and comfortable with the key tasks listed here.

Key Tasks

- Identify and build on the qualities and characteristics of youth including resiliency, coping skills, and protective factors.
- Identify and assist youth in developing systems of support, community resources, and social networks (e.g., family, friends, educators, employers, religious/spiritual advisors, groups, and other outside helpers and community members).
- Identify abilities and past solutions typically utilized in contexts other than the problem area(s) and link them to present situations.
- Learn what youth do to get their everyday needs met (i.e., whom they seek out for support, where they go for support).
- Identify moments (exceptions) in the past or present—even if fleeting—when the youth's problems were less present or absent altogether.
- Create opportunities for youth to acquire and develop new skills.
- Even when external influences factor into change (e.g., psychotherapy, medication, etc.) or youth assign change to influences outside of their control (e.g., luck, chance), attribute the majority of change to their qualities and actions.
- When others closely aligned with youth have made positive contributions to their lives, share the credit for change with such persons.

14   *A Day in the Life*

- Explore ways that youth can extend change into other areas of life.
- Encourage personal agency and accountability.

Principle 2: The Therapeutic Alliance Makes Substantial and Consistent Contributions to Outcome

Primary Competency: Engage Youth Through the Working Alliance

Relationships are at the foundation of change in YFS, with over 1,100 studies on the relationship and alliance (Norcross, 2011). The alliance or "working alliance" is considered a broader representation of the therapeutic relationship and includes four empirically established components: (1) the client's view of the relationship (including perceptions of the provider as warm, empathic, and genuine); (2) agreement on goals, meaning, or purpose of treatment; (3) agreement on the means and methods to achieve goals; and, (4) accommodating client preferences. Each of these four components will be discussed in upcoming chapters. What is important to establish here is the significance of working *with* youth and their support systems—including all persons involved in service planning, interventions, and the like.

Terms such as "agreement" and "accommodation" are used to emphasize the collaborative qualities of YFS services. Collaboration with youth and others begins with an unwavering commitment to "do what it takes" to create "environments of involvement." Although not all decisions are democratic ones, the more youth are involved in services the more opportunities there will be to learn about their preferences, to accommodate those preferences, and to work together to achieve some agreed-upon end point.

Collaboration extends beyond involvement and is predicated on feedback, a component of the strengths-based definition introduced earlier in this chapter. Referred to as "real-time" feedback in the professional literature, feedback is a crucial mechanism for determining whether and to what degree services are both a good fit and benefit youth. By "good fit" we mean that the services with youth and supportive others are in line with the four empirically based components that make up the alliance. Do youth feel heard and understood? Are the goals and means to accomplish those goals acceptable to youth? And do youth feel their preferences have been at minimum acknowledged and when possible met? These types of questions are essential given that client (in this case youth) ratings of the therapeutic relationship are widely considered the best and most consistent process predictors of improvement (Bachelor & Horvath, 1999; Baldwin, Wampold, & Imel, 2007; Horvath & Bedi, 2002; Martin, Garske, & Davis, 2000; Orlinsky, Grawe, & Parks, 1994; Orlinsky, Rønnestad, & Willutzki, 2004). Youth who are engaged

A Day in the Life 15

and connected with YCWs and those affiliated with services are likely to benefit most.

Effective RYCWs continuously work on their relationships with youth, understanding the importance of forming stable connections. The most significant difference between average and above average RYCWs is in their ability to form, nurture, and sustain alliances with diverse youth. The following is a series of key tasks for engaging youth through the alliance.

Key Tasks

- Use active listening, attending skills to connect with youth while recognizing that caution toward professionals may be an appropriate response based on their past experiences.
- Collaborate with caregivers, family members, outside helpers, and community resources to create strong social networks and systems of support.
- Collaborate with youth in setting goals.
- Incorporate the views of involved helpers (i.e., extended family, social service workers, medical personnel, educators, law enforcement, educators) in setting goals and determining directions.
- Collaborate with youth on tasks to accomplish goals.
- Use respectful, non-depersonalizing, and non-pathologizing language when describing youth and the concerns of youth.
- Discuss with youth parameters of confidentiality and informed consent.
- Learn about the preferences and expectations of youth and as best as possible accommodate services to those preferences and expectations.
- Offer options and choices in services and processes.
- Learn and adapt to the ways in which youth use language.

Principle 3: Culture Influences and Shapes
All Aspects of Youths' Lives

Primary Competency: Convey Respect of
Youth and Their Culture

To understand youth it is necessary to consider the cultural influences that shape their lives. Culture refers to a system of shared beliefs, values, customs, behaviors, and artifacts among various groups within a community, institution, organization, or nation. Hays (2007) suggests the acronym ADDRESSING as a way to identify different aspects of culture: age, developmental and acquired disability, religion, ethnicity, social class, sexual orientation, indigenous heritage, national origin, and gender/ sex. Brown (2008) has expanded on Hays's perspective to include factors

16   *A Day in the Life*

such as other social locations, vocational and recreational choices, partnership status, parenthood (or not), attractiveness, body size and shape, and state of physical health. Culture is a powerful filter through which youth can be understood.

Residential care is a context for RYCWs to extend dignity and respect to youth, just as in many cultures elders teach these core values to their young (Bolin, 2006; Vilakazi, 1993). In doing so RYCWs help youth fully develop their potential (Seita, Mitchell, & Tobin, 1996). This point is especially critical given that youth growing up in out-of-home care tend to have fewer consistent figures from whom to learn the value of dignity and respect. Moved from place to place—also known as the "shelter shuffle"—these youth are afforded fewer opportunities to develop their abilities and have those abilities supported and nurtured.

In our work with youth, we emphasize awareness and learning, forming new patterns of response and ways to effectively apply those responses to appropriate settings. RYCWs with diverse backgrounds can draw on their experiences and their general cultural knowledge to match youth's ideas about problems, possibilities, and potential solutions. Thus, knowledge of different cultures and perspectives is beneficial because it allows RYCWs to view situations differently without having to align with any one viewpoint. This knowledge also brings with it an expanded repertoire of methods to use that may be helpful in delivering services. What follows is a series of 10 key tasks for attending to cultural influences.

Key Tasks

- Maintain self-awareness and sensitivity to one's own cultural heritage, background, and experiences and their influence on personal attitudes, values, and biases.
- Recognize limits of multicultural competency and expertise.
- Acknowledge that specific racial and cultural factors influence service-oriented processes—understand and respect client's cultural heritage and practices.
- Create safe and nurturing cultural, physical, psychological, and social environments and settings.
- Acknowledge and address issues related to cultural safety.
- Use person-first language.
- Acknowledge youth as teachers and experts on their own lives and experiences.
- Empower youth and others by using practices that identify and employ their unique capabilities.
- Identify, assess, address, and monitor barriers to services, particularly those cultural barriers associated with accessibility.
- Adapt to the diversity and cultural contexts of the individuals, families, and communities served.

A Day in the Life 17

Principle 4: Effective Services Promote Growth,
Development, and Well-Being

Primary Competency: Utilize Strategies That
Empower Youth and Improve Their Lives

An integral aspect of the deficit- and pathology-driven perspective adopted by many residential programs is a focus on explanations. In particular, it is believed that past, present, and potential future problems and behavior of youth can be explained through available theories, thereby providing an appropriate rationale for interventions. For example, if problems can be explained as biological (i.e., anxiety, depression, etc.), then there is sufficient justification for biological intervention (e.g., medication). Miller, Duncan, and Hubble (1997) have challenged this notion by describing the role of mental health professionals as one of enhancing "the factors responsible for change-in-general rather than on identifying and then changing the factors a theory suggests are responsible or causing problems-in-particular" (p. 127). Following suit, a collaborative, strengths-based approach is predicated on services that promote present and future growth, development, and well-being rather than searched to explain and justify what often translates to more of the same, one-size-fits-all services.

Any path toward growth, development, and well-being begins with ensuring that the basic needs of youth are met (Maslow, 1943). Basic needs include but are not limited to food, water, sleep, and safety. In residential programs RYCWs are largely responsibility for ensuring that youth get their needs met. It is unrealistic to expect youth whose basic needs are not at least minimally met to focus sufficient attention and energy on making and sustaining change in other areas of life (Bertolino, 2014).

Growth, development, and overall well-being represent the *benefit* of services. In turn, benefit is measured by outcome. We ask: Are the services we provide actually making a difference for youth? Whereas *goals* are descriptive and measurable, *outcomes* reflect a youth's subjective interpretation of the impact of services on the three areas of functioning outlined in the definition of a strengths-based perspective: individual, interpersonal, and social role. By "subjective" we mean youth or others' interpretations of the benefit of services. In sum, if services are beneficial, this benefit will be reflected through positive outcomes, which means services have been effective.

Terms such as "benefit," "outcome," and "effectiveness" draw attention to the importance of routine and ongoing "real-time" feedback. This means monitoring change continuously, beginning with the start of services. Research makes it clear that change begins early in services (Miller, Duncan, & Hubble, 1997). While some youth will respond and make appreciable gains more slowly, this appears to be more the exception

18 *A Day in the Life*

than the norm. For youth who experience meaningful change early on, the probability of positive outcome significantly increases (Haas, Hill, Lambert, & Morrell, 2002; Percevic, Lambert, & Kordy, 2006; Whipple et al., 2003). When youth show little or no improvement or experience a worsening of symptoms early in services, they are at significant risk for negative outcome (Bertolino, Bargman, & Miller, 2013; Duncan, Miller, Wampold, & Hubble, 2010).

Because RYCWs spend more time with youth than other professionals, they have more opportunities to learn from youth and others involved what minimally needs to happen in each interaction, shift, meeting, and throughout the course of services to bring about meaningful and noticeable improvement. Next is a list of 10 key tasks for promoting effective growth, development, and well-being.

Key Tasks

- Focus on meeting the basic needs of youth (i.e., food, water, sleep, safety).
- View meaningful change as attainable and problems as barriers to progress, not fixed pathology.
- View growth, development, and maturation as part of the change processes.
- Consider individual, interpersonal, and social role functioning as robust indicators of benefit of services.
- Focus on maximizing the impact of each interaction and/or session.
- Monitor change from the outset of services, recalling that change tends to occur early in services.
- Emphasize possibilities for change through a future focus.
- Explore exceptions to problems and how change is already happening with youth.
- Focus on creating small changes, which can lead to bigger ones.
- Use methods that contribute to the youth's sense of self-esteem, self-efficacy, and self-mastery.

Principle 5: Expectancy and Hope Are Catalysts of Change

Primary Competency: Demonstrate Faith in the Restorative Effects of Services

Perhaps the most understated aspect of residential services is the role of hope for *both youth and RYCWs*. An accompaniment to hope, expectancy is a multifaceted phenomenon that refers to belief and confidence in services as safe, credible, and effective. For youth and supportive others, expectancy translates to a belief that residential services will, at minimum, be safe and help with the situation at hand and, ideally, contribute

A *Day in the Life* 19

to lasting overall positive change. Research indicates that increased expectancy acts as a placebo to counteract demoralization, activate hope, and advance improvement (Frank & Frank, 1991; Miller, Duncan, & Hubble, 1997). For RYCWs, expectancy is also essential because it reveals beliefs about residential services and, in some instance, services to youth in general. As discussed earlier in this chapter, RYCWs need to have faith both in services and in youth. RYCWs and other providers' attitudes can promote or dampen hope. An attitude of pessimism or an emphasis on psychopathology or the long-term process of change, for example, can negatively affect hope. In contrast, RYCWs who have the attitude that positive change can occur even in difficult situations coupled with an emphasis on possibilities tend to instill and promote hope in every interaction, however brief or seemingly inconsequential.

RYCWs can actively promote hope by using person-first language; by engaging in conversations that highlight strengths, choices, and options; by providing rationale for services and specific methods or interventions; and by demonstrating interest in the effectiveness of services (Duncan, Miller, & Sparks, 2004). When it comes to hope, two things appear to matter most to youth: (1) a belief that they are in "good hands"—that they are or will be cared for by respectful, compassionate staff in safe environments; and, (2) that they will be treated with respect, that their voices will be heard (including preferences), and that they will be collaborated with on most significant decisions regarding their residential stay.

Expectancy and hope help illuminate faith in services and in the prospects of positive change for youth in residential care. What follows are key tasks to help instill hope and increase the expectations of positive change.

Key Tasks

- Maintain the belief that positive change is possible in all aspects of YFS.
- Demonstrate faith in youth and their caregivers to achieve positive change.
- Demonstrate faith in the restorative effects of services.
- Build on preservice expectancy (i.e., the expectations youth and others may have at the *start of services*).
- Create expectancy for change by focusing on what is possible and changeable.
- Believe and demonstrate faith in the procedures and practices utilized.
- Show interest in the results of the therapeutic procedure, orientation, or method.
- Ensure that the procedure or orientation is credible from the youth's or caregiver's frame of reference.

20   *A Day in the Life*

- Ensure that the procedure or orientation is connected with or elicits the youth's previously successful experiences.
- View youth as people, not as their problems or difficulties or in ways that depersonalize them.

Durrant (1993) stated, "The aim of residential treatment is that the young person and his or her family should be able to experience themselves as competent and successful" (p. 28). Each of the principles described here is singularly pivotal to that purpose; however, each principle is also connected to and reliant on the others. It is their collective influence that serves to undergird residential care and provide direction to RYCWs. The chapters that follow will involve an exploration of different ways that RYCWs can employ strengths-based principles in everyday practice.

2 Something to Believe In
Orienting Toward Possibilities

A collaborative, strengths-based approach hinges not only on a belief that changes are possible with youth in residential programs but that RYCWs play a significant role in facilitating those changes. To become fully active agents of change, RYCWs shift away from deficit, pathology, and explanations to strengths and positive future change. In this chapter we begin to put into action the collaborative, strengths-based principles described in the opening chapter.

What Walt Disney Knew: Creating Possibilities

One of the many creative thinkers whose ideas influenced the 20th century was Walt Disney. At the heart of the many original innovations that began with Disney was a vision. Whether creating cartoon shorts or full-length feature films or developing new forms of entertainment with theme parks, Walt was constantly exploring what was possible— beginning with a vision, which was fueled by unwavering curiosity (and often tempered by his brother, Roy). But just how important was vision to Disney's success?

When Disneyland was being constructed, Walt would often take park engineers to the site to discuss his ideas with them. During these meetings it was common for Disney to convey what he had planned for a certain attraction or aspect of the park, which was at times outlandish, and for one or more of the park engineers to say, "Walt, we can't do that. It won't work." But Walt was persistent. He had a vision of how he thought Disneyland ought to be and was prepared for such reactions. As a remedy, one of the strategies he would use was to ask the park engineers to kneel down to view some aspect of the park. He would then have the engineers tell him what they saw. Why? Because Disney felt it was a way to get the engineers to experience the perspective of the children who would be coming to the park. Once the engineers could see what the children would see, achieving Disney's vision would take on new meaning. Instead of speaking of what could not be done, the park engineers would set out to make the seemingly impossible, possible. Walt Disney knew the value of vision, time after time turning ideas into reality (Thomas, 1994).

22   *Something to Believe In*

What can we learn from this? First, although we are not building theme parks, similar to Disney, we are building institutions in which possibilities are the rule, not the exception. As discussed in Chapter 1, focusing on possibilities is not about downplaying problems. It is not about having youth recite affirmations, thinking positively, or "wishing on a star." Youth and their supportive others experience real pain and suffering including emotional, physical, and socioeconomic hardships. Instead, we acknowledge the difficulties youth face while simultaneously exploring possibilities for present and future change.

What Walt Disney seemed to know was the importance of having collective vision—without it Disneyland would not have been designed, been funded, been built, and thrived. Further, collective vision is a necessary starting point to create momentum. We cannot expect RYCWs and other YFS staff who do not know what they are trying to accomplish to feel empowered and purposeful in their actions if they feel directionless.

A second thing we can learn from Walt Disney relates to the first. For Disney and the park engineers to communicate effectively, a common language was needed. To do his part, Walt learned to read architectural plans and how the engineers communicated with each other. In turn, the engineers adopted much of Disney's vocabulary, which was rich with words such as "dream," "future," and "imagination." By understanding each other, both factions could work together to achieve the vision that became Disneyland.

RYCWs also rely on a common language—in this case, language that focuses on collaboration and strengths. The result is a foundation for constructive conversations that inspire and empower those involved, clarify vision, increase understanding of roles and responsibilities, and positively change lives, relationships, communities, and institutions. Let's now see how this works in residential settings.

From Pathology to Strengths: The Language of Change

Much of the training RYCWs receive emphasizes the inabilities, liabilities, weaknesses, and deficits of adolescents. From this perspective, a goal in residential services is to help youth overcome these deficits. It is an interesting idea. If only it worked. Not only does a pathology focus not work, but its impact can extend far beyond services provided in residential care. In some cases youth end up worse off than before they began services. This phenomenon is known as *iatrogenic injury*, which specifically refers to methods, techniques, assessments, and other provider-initiated processes that may cause harm (Bertolino & O'Hanlon, 2002).

But let's also consider the point that a focus on pathology can leave a wake of negative aftereffects that can follow youth for years to come. For example, pathology-based language can stigmatize youth and inhibit positive change when youth are seen as "maimed," "bad," or "incapable"

Something to Believe In 23

or their abilities are unrecognized or ignored. So how does this happen? It begins with language.

The primary way through which RYCWs and other professionals share information is language. In mental health and social services, language is a vehicle for transporting ideas, either closing down or opening up possibilities for youth. In this section we will explore the latter—ways in which language can advance conversations, assist with communicating what is right and what is working, and create opportunities for future change. Arguably, how RYCWs use language will be the largest determinant in their effectiveness. In other words, the better we are with language, the more options we will have to connect and build relationships with youth, identify strengths, create hope, and so on. A starting point then is for RYCWs to trade in those vocabularies that contain unhelpful, jargon-filled, and potentially disrespectful words that inhibit change for a strengths-based vocabulary that emphasizes human potential and possibility. For comparison, Table 2.1 provides illustrations of both pathology- and strengths-based vocabularies.

A strengths-based vocabulary invites RYCWs to reexamine and question what they believe about residential services, the idea of change, behavior, and youth in general. Just by changing how we talk about youth and their challenges, we can create new possibilities through conversation. Let's take this a step further by considering possible implications of our words by reflecting on the following questions:

- Is it important for me to have hope in my life?
- Do I want others to respect me as a person?
- Do I prefer for people to point out my "defects" and flaws, or would I prefer people highlight my assets and capabilities?
- Do I want others to understand me solely on what I've done in the past, or would I like them to know who I am now and who I aspire to be?
- Do I want to be in a position of trying to fix youth or trying to empower them to make their own changes?

What feelings or thoughts did you have as you reflected on the questions? What questions seem to resonate most with you? When we apply the two different perspectives on language to ourselves, the picture can look very different. And if you have personally experienced the effects of problem- or pathology-laden language, then this is familiar. By considering how language circumvents every aspect of life, we can raise our degree of empathy to youth and others and the ways they are marginalized through words alone.

But awareness is just the first step because awareness without action does little to change situations and lives. A subsequent step is to use strengths-based words to identify positive characteristics and qualities, describe behavior, and construct collaborative conversations. Table 2.2 further illustrates the differences between traditional, pathology-based conversations and collaborative, strengths-based conversations.

Table 2.1 Pathology and Stengths-Based Vocabularies

Pathology Based	Strengths Based	Pathology Based	Strengths Based
Fix	Empower	Cure	Growth
Weakness	Strength	Stuck	Change
Limitation	Possibility	Missing	Latent
Pathology	Health	Resist	Utilize
Problem	Solution	Past	Future
Insist	Invite	Hierarchical	Horizontal
Closed	Open	Diagnose	Appreciate
Shrink	Expand	Treat	Facilitate
Defense	Access	End	Beginning
Expert	Partner	Judge	Respect
Control	Nurture	Never	Not yet
Backward	Forward	Limit	Expand
Manipulate	Collaborate	Defect	Asset
Fear	Hope	Rule	Exception

Table 2.2 Differences Between Traditional, Pathology-Based Conversations and Collaborative, Strengths-Based Conversations

Pathology-Based Conversations	Strengths-Based Conversations
Conversations for explanations	**Conversations for change/difference**
• Searching for evidence of functions for problems	• Highlighting changes that have occurred in youth's problem situations
• Searching for or encouraging searches for causes and giving or supporting messages about determinism (biological/developmental/psychological)	• Presuming change will and is happening
• Focusing or allowing a focus on history as the most relevant part of the youth's life	• Searching for descriptions of differences in the problem situation
	• Introducing new distinctions or highlighting distinctions with youth
• Engaging in conversations for determining diagnosis, categorization, and characterization	**Conversations for competence/abilities**
• Supporting or encouraging conversations for identifying pathology	• Presuming youth competence/ability
	• Searching for contexts of competence away from the problem situation
	• Eliciting descriptions of exceptions to the problem or times when youth dealt with the problem situation in a way they liked
Conversations for inability	
• Searching predominantly or exclusively for what youth cannot do and lack in terms of skill or ability	**Conversations for possibilities**
	• Focusing the conversation on the possibilities of the future/goals/visions
Conversations for insight/understanding	• Introducing new possibilities for doing/viewing into the problem situation
• Focusing primarily or exclusively on insight	

(Continued)

Something to Believe In 25

Table 2.2 (Continued)

Pathology-Based Conversations	Strengths-Based Conversations
Conversations for expressions of emotion • Focusing primarily or exclusively on elicitation of youth's expressions of feelings and on feelings	**Conversations for goals/results** • Focusing on how youth and caregivers or supportive others will know that they've achieved their therapeutic goals
Conversations for blame and recrimination • Making attributions of bad/evil personality or bad/evil intentions	**Conversations for accountability/ personal agency** • Holding youth and caregivers or supportive others accountable for their actions • Presuming actions derive from youth's intentions/selves
Adversarial conversations • Believing that youth and/or caregivers or supportive others have hidden agendas that keep them from cooperating with treatment goals/ methods • Using trickery/deceit to get youth to change • Believing that residential and other professional staff are experts and youth and caregivers or supportive others are nonexperts	**Conversations for actions/description** • Channeling the conversation about the problem situation into action descriptions • Changing characterizational/ theoretical talk into descriptive words • Focusing on actions youth and caregivers or supportive others can take to make a difference in the problem situation

To deepen our understanding of how the differences between pathology- and strengths-based conservations might appear in a residential setting, let's review examples of each. First is a dialogue between a RYCW and a youth that reflects the former:

RYCW: Welcome to our program, Craig.

YOUTH: Thanks.

RYCW: My name is Daryl. Where did you come from?

YOUTH: The Shelton Center. I hated that place.

RYCW: What didn't you like about it?

YOUTH: Everything.

RYCW: [Looking through the youth's file] It says in your file you came here because you got in two fights there. What was that all about?

YOUTH: I said I didn't like it there. Everyone was mean.

RYCW: Did you try to get kicked out?

YOUTH: No.

RYCW: What happened then, Craig?

YOUTH: I don't know. Why do we have to talk about this?

26   *Something to Believe In*

RYCW: It says that you're on Ritalin and Clonidine for ADHD [attention deficit hyperactivity disorder] and Abilify for depression. Were you taking your medication?

YOUTH: What?

RYCW: Your medication, were you taking it as prescribed?

YOUTH: Yeah, but it didn't help. It just made me sleepy.

RYCW: We'll have that fixed when you see your psychiatrist. Okay?

YOUTH: I guess.

RYCW: You know, we're not the bad guys here.

YOUTH: That's what they said at the last place.

RYCW: All right, well, I don't know what it was like at the Shelton Center, but I need to make sure you learn the rules. Okay?

YOUTH: Whatever.

RYCW: Like I said, we're not the bad guys. I'm not trying to make things more difficult for you. There are rules everywhere.

YOUTH: I know there are. It's like home but ten times worse.

RYCW: In your file it says you had trouble at home too. Is that right?

YOUTH: My mom didn't want me there after her new boyfriend moved in.

RYCW: I'm sorry about that. That must have been hard.

YOUTH: It still is.

RYCW: And since then you've been in four placements, and it says here in two of them you got in trouble for arguing with staff and having a bad attitude. Do you understand what you did wrong in those places?

YOUTH: Nobody would listen to me there.

RYCW: We'll listen to you here. Don't worry about that. But we've still got rules, so arguing and fighting will only make things worse. Here's a list of the rules. Let me know if you have any questions.

Let's now explore how the previous interaction could have gone differently using collaborative, strengths-based language:

RYCW: Welcome to our program, Craig.

YOUTH: Thanks.

RYCW: My name is Daryl. I'm a residential youth care worker here. You can call me Daryl or Mr. D., whichever you are comfortable with. So where'd you come from?

YOUTH: Mars.

RYCW: [Laughing] Ah, you're quick! Humor is something we appreciate around here! So, it says here in your file you came from the Shelter Center. What was that like?

YOUTH: I hated that place.

RYCW: I'm sorry to hear that. What was the hardest part for you?

YOUTH: Everything.

RYCW: We want this to be better for you. Were there one or two things that seemed to be harder than the others?

Something to Believe In   27

YOUTH: Everyone was mean—mostly the staff.

RYCW: I can assure you there are no mean staff here. And if your experience is different please let us know. We will treat you with respect but hold you accountable. Does that sound fair?

YOUTH: I guess.

RYCW: How long were you at the Shelton Center, Craig?

YOUTH: A year and a half.

RYCW: How did you manage to make it there so long?

YOUTH: I don't know.

RYCW: I was curious because you must have learned some things and done some things that helped you to be successful for that long.

YOUTH: But I got kicked out.

RYCW: Yeah, I know it didn't end too well. We can talk about that if you want to.

YOUTH: I don't want to.

RYCW: Okay. I read that you've been a few different places. I'm guessing you know quite a bit about residential programs—places like this. So maybe when you're up to it, you can tell me or other staff what worked for you or what helped you in some of those places. Is that cool?

YOUTH: That's cool.

RYCW: I think you can do well here. But it's what you think that matters most. Is there anything we can do for you now to help you feel more comfortable and to settle in?

YOUTH: I don't know. I'm not sure.

RYCW: No problem. It's a new place with new people and a lot to take in. There are always two staff around so just ask if you need something. Okay?

YOUTH: Okay.

RYCW: I have one more thing but, before we get to that, is there anything I forgot to ask about?

YOUTH: I don't think so.

RYCW: Do you have any questions?

YOUTH: Not right now.

RYCW: How about expectations? What expectations do you have for us?

YOUTH: [Shrugs his shoulders] I don't know.

RYCW: Well, Craig, you can expect and will receive from us a safe, clean place with enough to eat, warm water, and the things everyone should have. Staff will also treat you with care and respect. Does that sound okay?

YOUTH: It's good.

RYCW: Did I leave anything out?

YOUTH: I can't think of anything.

RYCW: Well, the last thing for now is the expectations we have of you. Yes, these are the rules, but we prefer to just call them "expectations." You won't remember them all right away so I am going to

28 *Something to Believe In*

give you this list to look over. [Hands youth a list of rules] Now I would bet that you are somewhat of an expert on rules since you've had them no matter where you've been. But for now I just want to cover one expectation. It's one that you can expect from us—respect. We ask that you respect us. Do you have any questions about what I mean by "respect"?

YOUTH: No, I know what you mean.

RYCW: Okay. We're glad you're here. Now let me show you around and introduce you to others.

YOUTH: Okay.

If the two conversations were to occur in real time, the differences would certainly be noticeable. But here we have the benefit of comparing transcriptions of them side by side. In doing so we can more readily identify the many differences in conversation. Let's begin with the first RYCW-youth interaction and its alignment with pathology-based conversations:

1. **Explanations, insight, and blame and recrimination**—"It says in your file you came here because you got in two fights there. What was that all about?"
2. **Blame and recrimination**—"Did you try to get kicked out?"
3. **Blame and recrimination**—"It says that you're on Ritalin and Clonidine for ADHD [attention deficit hyperactivity disorder] and Abilify for depression. Were you taking your medication?"
4. **Inability and adversarial**—"We'll have that fixed when you see your psychiatrist."
5. **Explanations and inability**—"I don't know what it was like at the Shelton Center, but I need to make sure you learn the rules."
6. **Insight**—"Do you understand what you did wrong in those places?"
7. **Adversarial**—"But we've still got rules, so arguing and fighting will only make things worse. Here's a list of the rules. Let me know if you have any questions."

Now let's perform the same kind of text analysis with the second RYCW-youth interaction to see how it aligns with a strengths-based conversational style:

1. **Competence/abilities**—"Ah, you're quick! Humor is something we appreciate around here!"
2. **Possibilities**—"We want this to be better for you."
3. **Accountability/personal agency**—"We will treat you with respect but hold you accountable. And if your experience is different please let us know. Does that sound fair?
4. **Competence/abilities, change/difference, and actions/descriptions**—"How did you manage to make it there so long?"
5. **Possibilities**—"I think you can do well here."

Something to Believe In 29

6. **Competence/abilities** and **change/difference**—"I was curious because you must have learned some things and done some things that helped you to be successful for that long."
7. **Competence/abilities**—"I'm guessing you know quite a bit about residential programs—places like this. So maybe when you're up to it, you can tell me or other staff what worked for you or what helped you in some of those places."
8. **Accountability/personal agency** and **competence/abilities**—"Yes, these are the rules, but we prefer to just call them 'expectations.' You won't remember them all right away so I am going to give you this list to look over. Now I would bet that you are somewhat of an expert on rules since you've had them no matter where you've been. But for now I just want to cover one expectation. It's one that you can expect from us—respect. We ask that you respect us. Do you have any questions about what I mean by 'respect'?"

Why is it so critical that RYCWs use collaborative, strengths-based conversations? There are several reasons. The first is rather straightforward: It is not enough to simply believe in change. It is not enough to hold ideas about how to stimulate positive change in our heads. We must engage in conversations for change with youth and supportive others. A second reason is that language is like a virus—a contagious virus. When we introduce new and respectful ways of talking with and about youth, others often pick up on those conversations. A result is that others become more aware of the influence of language. Finally, study after study shows that when youth are asked, post-services, what made a positive difference, they routinely say things like, "They [staff] listened to me," "I was respected," "I felt included," and "I was treated like a person." These kinds of responses are the result of building alliances with youth. And the primary way to build alliances is through language.

The point of language arises over and over in residential settings. A challenge for RYCWs is to avoid the pull to join in on expeditions for *answers*. Unless there are clear biological propensities in play (e.g., a cognitive disability, traumatic brain injury, etc.), we can only speculate about the nature of a youth's difficulty. This does not stop some mental health professionals from using their "expertise" to turn speculation into *unfounded fact*. In such cases problems are often created though language. Our aim has to be different. We create possibilities, instead of problems, by our words.

When we use collaborative, strengths-based language, we have more options for creativity. For example, write down as many options as can you think of for working with a youth who has been labeled as "hyperactive" or "argumentative" or "manipulative." Now, write down as many options as you can for working with a youth who "has a lot energy," "openly expresses herself," or "is a creative thinker." What becomes clear is the way we use language dramatically influences options for helping youth. RYCWs can use language that either closes down possibilities, as with "problem-talk," or

30 *Something to Believe In*

Table 2.3 Examples of Solution-Talk to Reframe Common Concerns Typically Described Through Problem-Talk

Problem-Talk	Solution-Talk
Hyperactive	Very energetic at times
Attention deficit disorder	Short attention span sometimes
Bipolar	Has significant ups and downs
Anger problem	Gets upset sometimes
Depressed	Sad
Oppositional	Argues a point often
Rebellious	Developing his/her own way
Codependent	People are important to him/her
Disruptive	Often forgets the rules in class
Family problems	Worries about his or her own life
Dissociative	Protects self emotionally when feeling unsafe
Shy	Takes little a time to know people
Negative peer pressure	People try to influence him/her
Isolating	Likes being by himself/herself

opens them up through "solution-talk" (Furman & Ahola, 1992). Table 2.3 provides examples of ways that we can use solution-talk to reframe common concerns that are typically described through problem-talk and in pathological terms.

A colleague of mine, Linda Metcalf (1995), has stated, "[People] often feel more *heard* when their problem is redescribed, and relax at the suggestion that things are not as bad as they thought. Describing a problem as terrible and difficult rarely motivates people to change" (p. 39). It is clear that how we talk has a direct impact on how we approach problems, possibilities, and solutions. A suggestion is that, as RYCWs, we use language to open doors to new possibilities while simultaneously holding youth accountable for their actions. This possibility-accountability duo is necessary regardless of whether a youth is in a residential center, an independent living program, outclient or outpatient services, a drop-in center, or another setting in which youth are served.

Personal Philosophy and Language: Self-Reflection in Action

Many of the youth we see in our residential programs have internalized stories that they are bad, defective, damaged, or just "no good." Most often these stories have evolved over time. There are instances, however, when the interactions youth have with staff in our programs contribute to them feeling that something is wrong with them. It's not that staff intend to contribute to or reinforce negative stories. As in the first RYCW-youth

Something to Believe In 31

dialogue earlier in this chapter, sometimes staff hold perspectives that are more pathology driven. In other cases staff communicate negative views without even knowing.

I once observed an interaction between a RYCW and a youth in which the RYCW said, "You shouldn't be such a control freak. You're going to lose all your friends. No one wants to be around someone like that." When I talked with the RYCW, named Todd, about the exchange and what he was hoping would arise out of the conversation, he stated that the youth he was talking to had been "barking orders at the others" as a group of youth played a board game. The conversation continued:

TODD (RYCW): I just didn't want him to lose more friends.
BB (BOB BERTOLINO): What were you hoping for instead?
TODD: That Derek [the youth] would have friends and keep them.
BB: I could tell you were looking out for him. I'm not sure that your concern for him came across in the way you'd hoped. Can you think of a different way of helping Derek? A way that would be more supportive and helpful to him.

Todd thought about what he could say. I encouraged him to take his time. Reflection is a crucial part of learning. A smile grew on Todd's face, and he continued the conversation.

TODD: The first thing is I would pull Derek aside—not in an embarrassing way—but maybe I would say, "Can I have your help for a second?" I shouldn't have tried to talk to him while he was in the group. I hope I didn't embarrass him. Then I would say, "You're funny and kind to everyone here. I think others want to be more your friend. I've got some ideas about how to help you with that. What do you think?"

I couldn't help but smile at Todd as I followed up.

BB: What you just described—it's terrific! You won't always have a lot of time to reflect in the moment, so you will have to do the best you can. But when you can take a few minutes to think about what you want to say before you say it, it usually comes across better. No matter what, afterward, always reflect. That way you will be able to evaluate what happened—what worked, what did not, and what you can do different the next time.

Todd brought our conversation to a close with a good self-observation:

TODD: With Derek I just did what I've been doing since I became a youth care worker. I never thought about it at the last place I worked, and no one said anything to me. Everyone was negative. That's why I left.

32   *Something to Believe In*

But I was part of that. I'm here because I believe in our kids. They are awesome. I will let them know that. I wish I had had this conversation a long time ago!

Not all conversations with staff will be similar to the one with Todd. In fact, when the issue of how residential staff communicate and how language is used is raised, it is not unusual for there to be defensiveness. I have heard things like, "We/I would never tell a kid they are no good" or "We/I don't use negative labels. We/I know better." The fact is that *all of us* sometimes come across in ways that we did not intend.

So our first task is to drop the defensiveness and self-reflect. When youth are interpreting interactions, like each of us, they are doing so through their cumulative experiences. And if those experiences have been largely negative, there is much more room for misinterpretation. Self-reflection is one way to deepen our understanding of this point so we can then focus on what *we can do as RYCWs* to use language more effectively.

Returning to the conversation just a short time ago, Todd had a personal philosophy (see Chapter 1) that included a belief in the potential of youth. His challenge was to use language that reflected his personal philosophy. He had the words but was not using them. If we are going to be effective as RYCWs or in any position in residential care, we need the formidable combination of personal philosophy and language. Both are essential in neutralizing and changing the negative, problem-saturated stories youth have about themselves and in creating the kind of culture we want in our programs. And with strengths-based culture, we can positively affect lives, just as Walt Disney did.

There's No Place Like Home: Envisioning Our Residential Programs

Looking at the Disney Company today, it is difficult to imagine the struggles Walt and his older brother, Roy, and their three siblings faced growing up in the Midwest in the early 1900s. They came from meager beginnings, faced economic hardships, and encountered significant family stress. At one point or another, each of the four Disney boys ran away from home due to conflict with their father, Elias. Eager to get away from home and join his brother Roy, who was fighting in World War I, at age 16 Walt tried to enter the army but was denied due to his age. This did not deter Walt, who instead was accepted into the Red Cross' Ambulance Corps and subsequently traveled overseas for the war.

After the war, the challenges continued for Walt as he tried to carve out a niche and career in animation—an industry in its infancy. The road included heartbreak, frustration, and more failures than successes. Walt was fortunate to have Roy as a copartner, who time after time managed to keep the company from bankruptcy, but just barely.

Following a string of successes with animated features such as *Snow White and the Seven Dwarfs*, *Pinocchio*, *Fantasia*, *Bambi*, and *Cinderella*, Walt conceived what would become his greatest accomplishment to date—Disneyland. In the face of the challenges to his vision, financial pitfalls, and struggles with technology that were so advanced, Disney prevailed. On July 17, 1955, the gates to Disneyland opened. During his dedication speech, Walt said:

> To all who come to this happy place: Welcome. Disneyland is your land. Here, age relives fond memories of the past, and here youth may savor the challenge and promise of the future. Disneyland is dedicated to the ideals, the dreams, and the hard facts that have created America, with the hope that it will be a source of joy and inspiration to all the world.

Notice that Disney referred to the park as "your place." He also made reference to "fond memories of the past" and "the challenge and promise of the future." And last, Walt chose words that symbolized what he believed best described Disneyland: "ideals," "dreams," "hope," "joy," and "inspiration." It is that kind of vision—a vision of the future and how things *can be* as opposed to what they will not be.

There is an inherent risk in making analogies, such as that of Disneyland and residential programs. Of course, in so many ways, they are markedly different. But all successful nonprofits and residential programs evolve from dreams and hopes that the lives of others can be better—and if not for the long-term, at least for the time those in our programs are with us. We have to establish cultures and environments that help youth experience hope, feel inspired, and achieve their futures.

The Pillars of Positive Deviance: Cultures of Excellence

Successful residential programs are built on three "pillars of positive deviance": YCWs (RYCWs in this instance), teams, and agencies (Bertolino, 2014). *Positive deviance* is a phrase used to describe those persons or groups that break from conventional ideals, often against great odds, for the betterment of others. The phrase evolved out of the work of Jerry and Monique Sternin, who were involved with several Vietnamese villages through the Save the Children Campaign (Pascale, Sternin, & Sternin, 2010). The Sternins helped the villages reduce rates of child malnutrition by identifying "positive deviants"—those families in which there were children who were well-nourished. Through close observation the Sternins learned that in the positive deviant families there were unique practices such as adding tiny shrimp and crabs and sweet potato greens to meals and feeding their children small meals three to four times a day, rather than bigger meals twice a day. Although these practices

34 *Something to Believe In*

were not customary in that part of the world, it was the seemingly small deviations that accounted for better nourished children. And because the deviations came from the villagers—not from outside entities—they were more sustainable.

We will continue to explore the first pillar, how RYCWs rely on positive deviance. The second pillar, teams, is equally important in residential care. Without teams that work together toward a collective vision, residential care will be marginal. Chapter 4 will include in-depth discussion about teams. The third and final pillar is agencies. By agencies we mean residential programs as standalone entities and the larger institutions to which they often belong. For example, some residential centers are not connected to other programs—they are the agency. They have their own policies, procedures, and systems. For those residential programs that are part of larger institutions, the operating procedures may be the same or different than for the agency at-large. What seems to be important in either case is how programs and agencies create cultures of excellence, which at times requires deviating from the norm. And the norm in residential care *has been* the pathology-based paradigm.

Success Starts at Home

In the mid-1980s, New York City had a problem with graffiti in its subway cars. To remedy this the city set up a special shed to repaint the subway cars as soon as they were identified. Gradually all the subway cars were repainted. The graffiti dissipated. New York City then used the same approach aboveground with infractions such as public drunkenness, littering, and the like. What was previously overlooked was now dealt with swiftly. The result? Before long the crime rate began to fall dramatically, just as it had in the subway.

The approach employed by New York City follows a concept known as the *Broken Window Theory*. The theory holds that minor, unchecked signs of deterioration in a neighborhood or community could, over time, result in major declines in the quality of living. If a part of a town or city becomes rundown (e.g., has broken windows), then lawbreakers feel emboldened since it appears that no one cares and no one is enforcing laws. Crime increases because criminals believe enforcement will be overlooked or neglected. Although a wide variety of complex factors likely contributed to the decreases in crime in New York City, a few small but influential changes in the environment of the city seemed to allow these factors to "tip" into a major reduction in crime (Gladwell, 2000).

One way to understand the idea of positive deviance in creating cultures of excellence is by contrasting Disney's approach with the Broken Windows Theory. What Walt Disney knew, and expected until his passing in 1966, has since become a cornerstone of the Walt Disney Company, which today stands as the largest single-site employer in the United

States. The expectation is that every Disney theme park is clean, operational, and equipped with high-quality customer service. There is no room for broken windows.

In psychology there is a subset of research that involves the study of "site effects" (Greenberg, 1999). Focus is on how different variables such as clients' perceptions of engagement, staff, physical settings, and so on affect outcomes. Just as unrepaired broken windows can send a message that suggests lack of care, so can unkempt residential settings, inattentive residential staff, lax structure, and the like. The youth who come to our programs deserve more.

As RYCWs we can set the tone for the success we aspire to with ourselves, peers, and programs. We do this by first making sure we are clear on where we stand philosophically. We also embrace the principles that underscore successful services. In accordance with personal philosophy and strengths-based principles is language. Because we pay close attention to what we say, to our language and how we engage youth in conversation, we learn something new every day. And finally, we explore every aspect of our settings to make them culturally safe, positive programs. As we will learn throughout the remainder of this book, similar to self-reflection, program evaluation is an ongoing process. There are no shortcuts to excellence. In the next chapter, we will begin our path toward excellence by exploring initial interactions with youth as they enter our residential programs.

3   Making Contact
Creating a Respectful Climate

Now that we have learned about the importance of using collaborative, strengths-based language to facilitate growth, development, and positive change with youth in residential programs, it's time to put what we have learned to work. We begin this chapter by exploring how the "first impressions" of youth and RYCWs influence initial contacts. We'll then explore how RYCWs can engage youth in ways that open up possibilities in initial contacts such as crisis hotlines and face-to-face assessments.

First Impressions

My very first shift as a RYCW was memorable. Because I was new, I was on shift with two other experienced RYCWs so that I could "learn the ropes." I thought I would be mostly observing and gradually easing my way into the mix. No such luck. Just a few minutes after my shift began, it was suggested that I "get my feet wet" by interacting with the youth. So I tried to enter the kitchen, where a few youth had gathered, as inconspicuously as possible. I didn't want to be too noticeable, as if I was carrying a sign saying, "New Guy!" It didn't matter—the residents saw me right away and zeroed in.

The first to greet me was a female resident.

"You're staff, right?" she observed. "You're new too."

Is it that noticeable? I wondered to myself.

"How do you know?" I nervously inquired.

"I've been here three weeks, and I know all the staff. I ain't never seen you. You must be new."

As she spoke two other youth joined in. Huddled in a semi-circle, my initiation began.

"How long you been here?" spouted the young girl, who appeared to be 14-ish.

"Not long," I replied.

After sizing me up a bit more, the teen snapped back, "We could jump you right now and there isn't anything you could do."

This was hardly what I expected. But I'd been jumped before, so I could feel my blood pressure rising. I gave notice that that this would not be a good choice.

I said, "That's a pretty bold thing to say when you don't know the first thing about me."

A second youth, a young man who was standing to my right, then became the voice of reason. "Yeah, you don't know nothin' about him. What if he knows karate or something?"

I thought to myself, that was a good call. And I had seen *The Karate Kid* at least a dozen times. Surely I could've pulled off a move or two as convincingly as Ralph Macchio—even without Mr. Miyagi's help.

The ringleader—the one who began my initiation—chuckled. "I was just kidding. We wouldn't jump you."

I wasn't completely convinced, so I stood still and stared back.

After a few moments of silence, I said, "How many friends does that strategy get you? It's pretty lame. How about we try a different one? I'm Bob. Who are you guys?"

The initiator was Crystal. Antwon, the voice of reason, was the male. The third teen, who had been silent during the exchange, was LaShonda.

LaShonda had apparently been studying the whole scene. She piped in, "Do you really know karate?"

"I guess you'll have to get to know me to find that out," I suggested.

That is how I was christened as a RYCW.

I have been in YFS for over two decades and have not had a greeting that parallels that first one as a RYCW. Because RYCWs are often the first contacts that youth have when entering placement, we will experience situations in which youth are angry, sad, frustrated, sarcastic, and so on. We have to keep in mind that it's not personal. Because so many youth have suffered and are merely trying to take care of themselves and survive, they will exhibit a wide range emotions, thoughts, and behaviors. In turn, RYCWs have their own experiences that, left unchecked, can influence the course of services. Let's explore this point further from the perspectives of both youth and RYCWs and the implications that each potentially brings forth.

Youth: "All These Places Are Alike"

For some youth the experience of a residential setting will be alarmingly new. They won't have seen anything like it. There will also be youth who have been in many residential programs, some beginning at a very young age. Residential staff often refer to these youth as doing the "shelter shuffle." Some youth have been in so many facilities that they can anticipate how RYCWs and other staff will respond to them during their stays. These youth may referred to as "treatment savvy" when the reality is that *they have been treated similarly at different places*. A result is youth

38 *Making Contact*

can start to feel that all facilities are the same—the same rules, the same level system, the same staff approach, the same consequences, and so on and so on. And as we have learned, there is good reason to feel that way because of the number of facilities that continue to institute traditional, pathology-driven models.

From a strengths-based perspective, we are deliberate in every effort to provide an altogether different experience for the youth in our programs. We don't just strive to dispel the myth of all facilities being the same; instead, we are proactive in creating respectful, healing environments. Doing so brings us back to the personal philosophies of RYCWs.

RYCWs: *"Here Comes Trouble"*

RYCWs are privileged to psychosocial evaluations, diagnostic assessments, and reports that present historical versions of a youth prior to even meeting that youth. In the best sense, these forms of information can provide RYCWs with perspective and perhaps a better understanding of a youth and his or her history. On the other hand, evaluations and assessments can serve as "rap sheets" that can shape the opinions of RYCWs. The following story illustrates the influence that historical information can have on the perceptions of RYCWs.

> I had been RYCW for just a few months when Matt arrived from placement in juvenile court facility. The 15-year-old had been assigned numerous psychiatric diagnoses including conduct disorder, bipolar disorder, and reactive attachment disorder, each of which was detailed in a dense file that accompanied him at the time of intake. Perhaps the most interesting description of Matt was by a psychologist who labeled him as having a "pathological personality." Matt earned this label because he laughed at things that others might not consider funny, made crude jokes, had a fondness for gory horror films, and had a "dislike of mornings."
>
> The descriptions of Matt weren't out of the ordinary for youth who came to the shelter. It was rare for us to receive documentation on youth that cast a positive light on them. But things were different—even experienced staff were nervous. It seemed the stories that accompanied Matt had taken on a life of their own. By the time I worked my first shift with Matt, I had heard various descriptions of him being "spooky" and "suspicious." I was nervous, and I had not even met Matt.

It is not information itself that is the problem, but instead *how information influences* RYCWs (and residential staff as a whole) and contributes to a "forecasting effect." This is when information is seen as reality—the way things are—which can contribute to unhelpful assumptions. In

Making Contact 39

turn, such assumptions can have predictive value. For example, a RYCW might think and even say, "This kid's got a history of problems wherever he's been. We're in for trouble," "He's been diagnosed with ODD [oppositional defiant disorder]. Don't be surprised if he argues and pushes us to the limit," or "She's been in detention three times. Her behavior problems aren't going to just go away."

What if RYCWs begin initial contacts with views similar to the aforementioned ones? How might those views influence first interactions? Conversely, if a youth behaves differently during the initial contact, will his or her history overshadow what the RYCW observes? Will RYCWs trust their own perspectives? Or will they assume youth are "just behaving" if they are friendly, respectful, agreeable, and so on? It would be understandable, for example, for a RYCW to think, "He's just putting on an act for us," "She's in a honeymoon phase," or "We'll see her real self soon enough." What seems clear is that initial interactions can both positively and negatively affect services.

It is clear that the lenses through which RYCWs peer are especially influential. Further, the messages that RYCWs convey to youth during initial contacts can set the tone for the entire course of placement. Thus, if RYCWs only see youth through the lens of previous case histories, a youth may have little chance to escape such negative and closed-down views. However, if RYCWs persist with personal philosophies that who youth are supersedes paper trails, the potential benefit of services increases, and the likelihood that youth will see themselves in more possibility-oriented ways increases. Let's return to the story of Matt.

> Because I had been off work, Matt had been in our program for two days before I met him in person. I cautiously waited for the Matt who was portrayed in the evaluations and reports to appear. It never happened. Instead, what I witnessed was a young man of few words—until he got to know you. Then the smiles and laughter came flowing out through infectious stories that revealed his hopes and dreams. Matt made no excuses for the behavior that led to his out-of-home placement. He sought only an opportunity to show others the kind of person he was. For me, that was the very reason residential programs existed—to help youth like Matt make the most out of new opportunities.
>
> Although our emergency shelter was a short-term program, an exception was made for Matt so that he did not need to do the shelter shuffle any longer before returning home. His stay was extended to two and half months, during which he excelled through the shelter's level system to the point that a new level had to be created to accommodate his growth. Matt completed work toward his GED (General Educational Development) and began to explore job options. And he took on a leadership role, assisting new residents with learning about and adjusting to the shelter program.

40   *Making Contact*

A couple of years after reuniting with his family, Matt returned as a peer volunteer with the agency. In this role he mentored shelter youth and provided support. And in a signature moment, Matt was selected to go with other agency staff to Washington, DC, to advocate for services to homeless and displaced youth at a conference. For years to come, people would talk about Matt's remarkable lobbying efforts.

Psychotherapy research demonstrates that service providers' attitudes, particularly in the opening moments of services, can greatly influence clients' expectations for change (Miller, Duncan, & Hubble, 1997). Applied to RYCWs, this means those who emphasize possibilities and the belief that things can work out help build hope. In contrast, an attitude of pessimism, an emphasis on psychopathology, or a focus on the long-term nature of change can have an adverse effect. Despite these findings, it is not uncommon for RYCWs to underestimate their impact on youth—not just during initial but in *all* interactions. Quite simply, perspective matters, and youth cannot afford our pessimism.

In Chapter 1 I spoke of surgeon Atul Gawande, who affirms hope for patients as a necessary quality for health-care providers. Few have touched on this point with more fervor than Emil "Jay" Freireich, who started college at the age of 16 with $25 given by a friend of his mother and began medical school at 18. Dr. Freireich helped discover the cure for childhood leukemia before he was 40. He became *the* champion of clinical research to alleviate the suffering of thousands of cancer victims. Dr. Freireich is very clear when he speaks about pessimism and hope:

> There's no possibility of being pessimistic when people are dependent on you for their only optimism. On Tuesday morning, I make teaching rounds, and sometimes medical fellows say, "This patient is eighty years old. It's hopeless." Absolutely not! It's challenging. It's not hopeless. You have to come up with something. You have to figure out a way to help them, because people *must have hope* to live.
> (quoted in Gladwell, 2013, p. 139)

There is an unmistakable truth when it comes to Dr. Freireich's position and YFS. There is no room for pessimism in what we do. We each have a responsibility to help and support youth, who are among the most marginalized in society. We must focus on what is possible and help youth reach their capacities to make better decisions, be responsible, and grow. If we do not believe in youth, who will?

Face-to-Face Information Gathering and Assessment

Youth are brought to residential programs by parents, caregivers, child protective and child welfare services workers, juvenile officers, and other law enforcement personnel (for example, when youth are placed in protective custody). A first step upon arrival is typically a face-to-face meeting—an intake assessment or interview. In many programs the intake process is merely a formality to gain further information as the youth has already been accepted into the program. In other settings initial face-to-face interviews are used to determine whether a youth is "appropriate" for admittance. This is because programs often have preset guidelines regarding which youth they will accept. For example, although some facilities will work with youth with histories of aggressive behavior, others will not.

An intake assessment or interview can take anywhere from 20 or 30 minutes to several hours, depending on the extent of the evaluation processes used and the criteria outlined for determining and/or completing admission. Sometimes youth will be seen with their family members or supportive others. It is also common for there to be multiple parts of initial interviews, with other people being present at some parts and not at others.

Intake assessment in residential settings can vary greatly in terms of process, but what tends to remain constant is an agency or program's philosophy. And while initial face-to-face interviews are important for gathering information, they need not be a method of pathology detection. Rather, initial assessments provide opportunities to connect with youth, identify strengths, and facilitate positive change processes.

The most important factor in facilitating positive change in residential services is the quality of relationships between RYCWs, youth, and supportive others. Recall the second strengths-based principle described in Chapter 1, *The therapeutic alliance makes substantial and consistent contributions to outcome*, and the associated key competency, *Engage youth through the working alliance*. As we have learned, research indicates that those who are engaged and connected with service providers benefit most from services; however, those who have worked as RYCWs do not need research to know this to be true. It is evident in every aspect of services. But what is especially important here is the perceptions youth have of RYCWs as being warm, empathic, trustworthy, and nonjudgmental (Norcross, 2011).

To engage youth and supportive others during initial face-to-face contacts, RYCWs can do the following:

1. Create Listening Space: Experience the Stories of Youth;
2. Engage Through Attending: Possibilities in Language;
3. Gather Information: Collaborative, Strengths-Based Questioning; and,
4. Gain Focus: Develop a Vision of the Purpose of Services.

Next we explore each of these components.

Create Listening Space: Experience the Stories of Youth

The very idea of residential treatment can evoke an array of emotions for youth and those who support youth. Along with feelings that youth may

42 *Making Contact*

be experiencing about the circumstances of their lives are the expectations of coming to a new place. Worry, fear, anger, disconnection, and resentment are but a few of the emotions commonly expressed either verbally or nonverbally during initial interactions. A good place to start, then, is by "creating listening space." Creating listening space is also a *collaboration key* (Bertolino, 2014). Collaboration keys enhance engagement by bringing youth and supportive others' expectations, preferences, and perspectives on change to the forefront of services. A comprehensive discussion of collaboration keys in YFS can be found elsewhere (see Bertolino, 2014).

To create listening space, we give permission for youth and supportive others to express themselves through their perspectives—their stories. By encouraging youth to start wherever they feel comfortable, we create opportunities to increase engagement through understanding how they see their lives and situations. We consider that, for some youth, being able to tell their stories will be the most valuable part of their time in our programs.

It is understood that the idea of demonstrating patience by not asking assessment questions right away may present conflict for RYCWs. This is in part because RYCWs are often trained to move conversations forward in a timely manner. After all, residential placements are busy places. Rushing through assessment processes and using "cookie cutter" methods, however, without adequately listening to youth is disrespectful and irresponsible. What is adequate? Saying to youth, "I want to be sure I hear your thoughts and feeling about being here. I also want to be sure to answer any questions you may have. If I happen to move too quickly or miss something, please let me know. And should you have questions later, don't hesitate to ask." This "open door" policy—a willingness to answer the questions youth have at any time during their stay in our programs—distinguishes better programs from average ones. And we want to be better than average.

Beyond being the right thing to do, good listening increases the chance that youth will talk about their lives and experiences. When youth engage in conversation, we are more likely to learn about their perceptions of problems, attempts at previous solutions, and what might work. We may also pick up hints as to what was helpful or unhelpful in their eyes in services in previous settings. With this information we have a better idea about what might help make the experience more beneficial to the youth. We can also reduce the likelihood that RYCWs will try to implement strategies that youth have found unhelpful and even disrespectful. For example, if a youth related that she struggled with female staff who spoke loudly because her mom used to yell at her, that would be helpful for staff in the new setting to know. The RYCW doing the intake might follow up by saying, "We have female staff on most shifts. Can you tell us what helps you feel more comfortable when female staff talk with you and, in particular, when they need to get your attention?"

A question arises: If we are creating listening space, how will we get the information needed to complete our assessments? The answer is that it is not necessary for youth and supportive others to go on endlessly during initial contacts. In fact, because careful listening actually increases disclosure from youth, RYCWs are able to gather information with fewer questions. Further, better relationships mean that when we do ask questions, those questions typically come across as less repetitive, invasive, and threatening. When youth feel heard and listened to, as if RYCWs are on their side, they are more willing to extend themselves when answering questions.

Engage Through Attending: Possibilities in Language

There exists a multitude of ways to engage youth, increase understanding, and open up future possibilities. This section presents two strategies that fall under an umbrella known as *Active Client Engagement* (ACE; see Bertolino, 2014). In general ACE refers to ways of using *language* and *interaction* to strengthen connections and facilitate change. *Language* is comprised of two forms of communication. The first is what is said verbally. The second is what is nonverbally communicated through voice tone, rate of speech, intonation of words, posture, and so on. To be effective RYCWs have to be attuned to both forms of communication. *Interaction* relates to the specific ways RYCWs engage youth. For example, RYCWs may use humor, storytelling, self-disclosure, and so on to strengthen connections. It is important that RYCWs maintain a posture of flexibility in adapting to the relational styles and preferences of youth, making adjustments based on what is communicated.

The concept of adjusting to relational styles is a fertile area of research. Evidence to date indicates that the most effective mental health professionals are the ones who are able to manage challenging interpersonal encounters (Anderson, Ogles, Patterson, Lambert, & Vermeersch, 2009). In other words, regardless of the way youth relate (i.e., passive, subdued, aggressive, dependent, etc.), effective RYCWs are able to find ways to connect and build rapport with youth. They learn over time "what to say, how to say it, and when to say it."

Another characteristic of effective RYCWs is that they keep things simple. They steadily focus on the healing effects of secure, safe relationships. Numerous studies have demonstrated the value of *empathy*, *positive regard*, and *congruence*. In general terms, *empathy* is a person's ability to understand another's perspective or way to experience the world. *Positive regard* is usually described as a person's warmth and acceptance toward the self or another. *Congruence*, sometimes referred to as genuineness, has been characterized by the helper's personal involvement in a relationship and willingness to share this awareness through open and honest communication. Important to bear in mind is that empathy, positive regard, and congruence all exist in the experience of those we

44 *Making Contact*

endeavor to help, which underscores the importance of feedback, which will be discussed in upcoming chapters.

Let's keep things simple to start by focusing on two ways to engage youth: *acknowledgment* and *validation. Acknowledgment* involves attending to what youth have communicated both verbally and nonverbally. It lets them know that their experience, points of view, and actions have been heard and noted. It also serves as a prompt by encouraging youth to continue communicating. A basic way to acknowledge is to say, "Uh huh" or "I see." Another way is to reflect back, without interpretation, what was said. For example, a RYCW might say, "You're angry" or "I heard you say you're sad." This can also be conveyed by attending to nonverbal behaviors. For example, a RYCW might say, "I noticed you clenched your fist as you talked about being in places like this" or "I can see the tears."

Validation is an extension of and is most often used in conjunction with acknowledgment. It involves letting youth know that whatever they are experiencing is valid. We want to communicate that youth are not bad, crazy, sick, or weird for being who they are and experiencing whatever goes on inside them. RYCWs can use validation to normalize the situation or convey that others have experienced the same or similar things. Validation is commonly expressed through statements such as, "It's/That's okay" or "It's/That's all right." To combine acknowledgment with validation, add words or statements such as "It's/That's okay" or "It's all right" to what is being acknowledged. A RYCW using acknowledgment and validation might say, "It's okay to be angry," "It's all right if you're angry," or "I heard you say that you're sad, and you can just let that be there." Acknowledgment and validation are responses that should be used in all interactions.

Let's now learn two strategies for using language to engage youth. These strategies include *paraphrasing and summarizing* and *acknowledgment and possibility*. Each strategy is used purposefully by RYCWs to let youth know we are listening, to state that we have heard what they are saying, and to further the conversation. In addition, several strategies introduce the element of *possibility*, not as a form of direct intervention, but rather to create subtle inroads to future positive change.

Paraphrasing and Summarizing

If not through experience then surely through education, most RYCWs learn about acknowledgment and validation. There is no substitute for the two, which are used as a way of letting youth know we are not only paying attention, but also listening to what they have said. Two ways to express acknowledgment and validation are through paraphrasing and summarizing. These methods can be used in any form of conversation but are particularly important during initial contacts. This is because

Making Contact 45

youth and supportive others will tune us out if they sense we are glossing over their experiences. Next we explore examples of these two methods.

Paraphrasing can be used as a way to confirm what has been said by using a condensed, nonjudgmental version of what the youth or involved other has said.

Example 1   YOUTH: I'm sick of going from place to place.
RYCW: You're sick of going from one residential place to another.
Example 2   CAREGIVER: Kate does whatever she wants, whenever she wants. It's draining.
RYCW: You're feeling drained by Kate's actions.

Summarizing offers a way to check out what has been said by pulling together what a youth or other has said over a period of time (i.e., a few minutes of conversation or different segments from different points of a conversation). Summarizing provides a brief synopsis to acknowledge, clarify, and gain focus.

Example 1   YOUTH: [End of a lengthy statement] . . . that's about it. That's what's going on.
YCW: Let me see if I follow you. You mentioned several things. One is the arguing between you and Carrie [one of her roommates]. Another is that it seems you are worried about finding an independent living program by the time you turn 17. Is that right?
Example 2   YOUTH: . . . I feel like I could just keep talking about it but it wouldn't get me anywhere. My life is going backward, and there isn't anything I can do about it.
YCW: It certainly seems like you've been through a lot in a short period of time. First, you thought you were doing better in school than you were. And when you got your grades, you were shocked. And on top of that, two people who you've been close to here have left the program.

Acknowledgment and Possibility

Acknowledgment and validation through paraphrasing and summarizing are methods of effective listening. The more we practice, the more we develop them. There are, however, occasions in which acknowledgment and validation are not enough. If fact, for some youth, the more we acknowledge and validate, the more they will box themselves into corners through their words. All the pure reflection in the world will not change that.

One way to help youth out of the corners they have boxed themselves in is to introduce "possibility-talk"—a twist on pure reflection. Perhaps

46　*Making Contact*

you will recall the famous Warner Brothers cartoons involving Road Runner and Wile E. Coyote. In one particular episode, Wile E. Coyote sets a trap by painting a fake door and doorknob on the wall of a cave. When Road Runner enters the cave, Wile E. Coyote thinks he has finally caught his nemesis. But, of course, he hasn't. How does Road Runner escape? Even if you haven't seen the episode, you probably figured it out: He turns the fake doorknob to open the fake door and escapes. But what is important about Road Runner is he is always trying to find ways out of seemingly closed-down situations.

This very idea can be applied to our conversations with youth. We can use a twist to pure reflection to paint doorways with possibilities in otherwise closed-down statements. Next are three ways to do this.

1. *Use the past tense.* Repeat youth or others' statements or problem reports in the past tense to create subtle openings in their perspectives. If only acknowledgment is used, some will remain stuck. If only a search for possibilities occurs, some will feel invalidated. Using the past tense helps youth and others feel understood while suggesting that things can be different now or in the future.

Example 1　YOUTH: I'm in trouble a lot.
　　　　　　　RYCW: You've been in trouble a lot.
Example 2　CAREGIVER: She says means things to me.
　　　　　　　RYCW: She's said some mean things to you.
Example 3　CHILD SERVICES WORKER: He always makes bad decisions.
　　　　　　　RYCW: He's made some bad decisions.

During our interactions, when a youth or other gives a present-tense statement of a problem, we use paraphrasing or summarizing to acknowledge and reflect the statement back in the past tense. Doing so can offer the possibility of a different present or future. When RYCWs only acknowledge and validate, some will move on, but most will not. Youth will continue to describe situations as impossible and or unchangeable. Alternatively, some may feel that they are being pushed to move on or "get over it," which can be invalidating.

2. *Translate youth or others' statements into partial statements.* Translate their statements using words such as "everything," "everybody," "always," and "never" into qualifiers related to time (for example, "some things," "somebody," "sometimes," and "much of the time"), intensity (e.g., "a lot," "a bit less," "somewhat more"), or partiality ("a lot," "some," "most," "many"). RYCWs should take care not to minimize or invalidate youth or others' experiences.

Example 1　YOUTH: I get in trouble all the time.
　　　　　　　RYCW: You've been in trouble a lot.

Example 2   YOUTH: Nothing ever goes right for me.
            RYCW: Sometimes nothing's gone right for you.
Example 3   CAREGIVER: My son will never make friends because he treats
            everyone so badly.
            RYCW: Many have found it hard to be friends with your son
            because of how he has treated them.

All-or-nothing statements typically represent frustration and disappointment. But they also represent opportunities to interject possibilities because
they are global generalizations, they do not exist in the world. By using
qualifiers with acknowledgment—going from global to partial—we help
introduce the element of possibility while simultaneously acknowledging.
At the same time, if youth or others feel that their experiences are being
minimized or they are being pushed to move on, they will likely respond
with a statement such as, "Not sometimes, all of the time." If a youth or
other reacts in such a manner, the RYCW must make sure the youth or other
feels heard and understood by validating further while keeping an eye on
possibilities. For example, a RYCW might respond by saying, "I'm sorry I
misunderstood. Nothing has gone right for you." In this example the youth
perspective is acknowledged while also put into the past tense.

3. *Translate into perceptual statements.* Translate youth or others' state-
    ments of truth or reality—the way they explain things for themselves—
    into perceptual statements or subjective realities (for example, "in
    your eyes," "your sense is," "from where you stand," "you've gotten
    the idea").

Example 1   CAREGIVER: I'm clearly a bad mother because my kid's always
            in trouble.
            RYCW: In your eyes you're a bad mother because your kid's
            been in trouble.
Example 2   YOUTH: I'll never amount to anything.
            RYCW: Because of what you've done, it seems to you that
            you'll never amount to much.
Example 3   YOUTH: I keep getting bad grades in school. I'm never going
            to do any better.
            RYCW: Some poor grades have given you the idea that you
            won't do well in school.

It is common to combine multiple methods of acknowledgment and
possibility. In fact, the use of past tense is commonly combined with
the second and third methods, as evidenced by the examples provided.
And although the point here is show how we can change language in the
moment with youth and others, rarely do people consciously recognize
these changes. Rather, strengths-based conversations provide new ways
of talking about problems, which in turn offers possibilities for changing
perceptions self, others, and situations in the present and future.

48　*Making Contact*

Let's now see how the idea of creating possibilities can be applied in an initial contact. The following example is of a 12-year-old named Will, who was brought to a short-term residential program by his mother after stealing the family car and running away. Will's mother was concerned that she could not control her son and sought a family time-out to figure out what to do next. After introductions, the RCYW, the mother, and Will had the following conversation.

RYCW: Where would you like to begin?

MOTHER: Everything's such a blur. I mean, I thought things were fine and then all of the sudden he steals the car and takes off. And then he ran away again right after that.

RYCW: It sounds like you and your family have been through a lot. And until recently things seemed to be moving along just fine—then the several things happened. Is that right?

MOTHER: Exactly. I still don't know where he got the idea to steal the car. That was just plain dumb! Then he ran away. I have no idea what's going on. It's scaring me. We had to do something.

RYCW: I understand. And you've been wondering where the ideas came from to take the car and then run away. What's the scariest part of what's happened?

MOTHER: I'm afraid he's going to end up in more trouble and maybe even locked up for good.

RYCW: You're worried because he's done some things that would lead just about any parent to believe that their son or daughter might be heading for more trouble, including the possibility of being locked up. [Mother nods her head yes.] That is scary.

MOTHER: Really scary.

RYCW: Is that what you are most concerned about—Will being locked up?

MOTHER: Definitely.

RYCW: [Speaking to Will] Will, how do you see things?

WILL: She gets mad at everything.

RYCW: So it seems to you that your mom gets mad at you a lot—because of things you've done.

WILL: I guess.

RYCW: Can you give me an example?

WILL: I don't know. She's on my case about different stuff—mostly my friends. She never lets me see them.

RYCW: There are a few different things in your eyes, but the main thing for you is your friends—wanting to see them more often.

WILL: For sure.

This brief transcript began with the RYCW creating listening space and then using language to enhance engagement and open possibilities in closed-down statements. Both the mother and Will were offered opportunities to share their perspectives while the RYCW used possibility-talk to acknowledge and create openings for future change. First and foremost it is important that each person feels heard and understood. Next, we do not want youth or others involved to feel that the conversation is rushed or that problems are being glossed over, which can contribute to a sense of invalidation. Instead our aim is to engage in helpful conversations that encourage, promote hope, and facilitate positive change.

Learning to use language in new ways is not an easy thing. It takes ongoing effort and reflection. So again, it is necessary that RYCWs practice with changing language to increase automaticity. Practice will also contribute to greater comfort and consistency in identifying and attending to words, phrases, and statements that suggest impossibility.

Gather Information: Collaborative, Strengths-Based Questioning

Most residential programs use standardized forms to gather information. In a growing number of settings, electronic record-keeping systems are used while others rely on paper forms, and some use both. There are also substantial variations regarding the type of information gathered. Minimally, programs will secure demographic data and a brief social history. Due to licensing and funding requirements, many programs will employ lengthy, in-depth information-gathering procedures that include complex forms of assessment, more often than not used to diagnose or label. And because of the influence of the pathology-based perspective, DSM (*Diagnostic and Statistical Manual of Mental Disorders*; see American Psychiatric Association [APA], 2013) diagnosis and labels such as SPMI (severe and persistent mental illness) and SED (severely emotionally disturbed) are commonly required for reimbursement; due to this, residential staff may feel that their hands are tied when it comes to gathering information during initial contacts.

As research has demonstrated the importance of focusing on the strengths and resources of youth and strengthening relationships—the principles outlined in Chapter 1—more innovative ways of gathering information during initial contacts have become available. The result is more balanced approaches to both understanding problems—which often bring youth to our programs—and ways of identifying and building on strengths. In this way, information gathering or assessment, as it is more commonly known, is not an "either/or" but a "both/and" proposition. In order to understand youth, their situations, and their lives, we need to know about challenges (problems and concerns) and possibilities (strengths and solutions).

A starting point is for RYCWs to first know whether they are "screening in" or "screening out." From a strengths-based perspective, this means

50 *Making Contact*

to figure out ways we can serve more youth, not keep them from our programs. This is a philosophical point to be determined before information gathering begins. Next, RYCWs want to become familiar with the requirements of their settings. Familiarity will help with identifying places that a strengths-based perspective can be interwoven into already existing practices. Another point is for RYCWs to be clear on their personal philosophies. Doing so will reduce the likelihood that initial contacts, and, in particular, information-gathering processes, leave youth and those in support of youth feeling worse than they did before the interaction began.

Next, RYCWs can further engagement by talking with all present about the overall process:

> There are some questions that I am going to ask that we ask of all who come here. First I'll ask you a few questions that will tell me what's been happening that's a problem or at least concerning. Once we get through those questions, we'll move on to some others that will tell me more about what you do well and what has been going well, maybe even working, even just a little bit.

As discussed, many standardized assessments may be pathology- or problem-focused but still allow room for RYCWs to ask questions to evoke competencies and resources. For example, first the RYCW asks about the overall concern or problem, including when it is most intrusive, disturbing, and so on. Then the RYCW explores exceptions to the concern or problem, including when things are going *just a little better* or the problem is absent altogether and what is different about those times. Here is an example of how this might look in practice:

RYCW: Cedric, tell me a bit about school. Which school do you attend?
CEDRIC (YOUTH): Abbott [Middle School].
RYCW: What grade are you in?
CEDRIC: Seventh.
RYCW: What's school like for you?
CEDRIC: It's stupid.
MOTHER: He's failing everything—all his classes. That's part of the problem.
CEDRIC: I'm not failing all my classes!
RYCW: Really? Please say more about that.
CEDRIC: I'm passing science and gym. I've got a C in science and a B in gym.
RYCW: Wow! [To the mother] What is your take on this?
MOTHER: Well, yeah, I guess he is passing those two.
RYCW: [To Cedric] I am fascinated by this. So even though you have struggled with a few of your classes, in two of them you are passing—science and gym. How have you managed to do that?

CEDRIC: I don't know.

RYCW: What have you done differently in those two classes?

CEDRIC: I have to go to gym.

RYCW: Sure, you have to go. Are you required to dress out and participate?

CEDRIC: Yeah.

RYCW: Hmm. Well, I've heard from youth who don't dress out and participate even if it means failing. And so I'm curious, how do you get yourself to do that when maybe sometimes you don't feel like it or want to?

CEDRIC: I just do.

RYCW: What about science? How have you managed to hold a C?

CEDRIC: Sometimes I do good on tests.

RYCW: That's fantastic. Is it that you are a good test taker, or is it something about science or maybe something else?

CEDRIC: I like science so I listen more.

RYCW: I see. Science is more interesting so you pay closer attention. And do you take notes?

CEDRIC: No, I just remember it.

RYCW: That is quite an ability. And it has me thinking a few things. The first is that when you commit to something—like going to gym, dressing out, and participating—it pays off with a better grade. The second thing is you are good at retaining and recalling information when it is interesting to you—like in science. And this has me wondering: How might you use your abilities just a little more in your other classes—just enough to pass? You may or may not know the answer right now. And if you don't, it may come to you later. In either case you seem to know something about what to do to improve things academically for yourself.

Even when situations seem problematic, RYCWs ask, "What else?" We search for exceptions to problems. Exception-oriented questions are a core form of collaborative, strengths-based questions as a whole and involve exploration of times when problems seem less dominating, occur less frequently, are absent, and the like. Information gathered then forms building blocks for future change.

As evidenced by the previous case example, it is helpful, but not necessary, for youth or others involved to know the answers to exception-oriented questions. In fact, many youth will reply with "I don't know" when faced with such questions. The value of exception questions is they create attention around the "What else?" of problems. In other words just by asking such questions we orient youth and others' attention to "What's right?" including what is working, has worked, and/or may work in the future. What follows are examples of questions that can help with the search for exceptions:

52   Making Contact

- When does the problem seem less noticeable to you? What are others doing when the problem is less noticeable?
- When does the problem seem to happen less?
- What do you suppose keeps you from going off the deep end with trouble?
- What is it like when the problem is a little less dominating?
- What is happening when things are a bit more manageable regarding the problem?

Notice that the aforementioned questions do not inquire about extremes. We don't ask, "When don't you have the problem?" That's too big a leap for most youth and their systems of support. Our aim is to elicit small exceptions. We search for the topography of problems to find the proverbial needle in a haystack, a ray of light in a dark sky. Exceptions not only represent opportunities to facilitate present and future change, they also increase hope, which is especially important in residential programs, which almost always begin under negative circumstances.

Now let's consider a few of the areas that are typically a focus of information gathering in residential programs. Each area includes examples of exception-oriented questions:

Problem/Situation

- When does the problem or concern that brought you here seem a little less noticeable to you?
- Tell me about a time recently when things went a little bit better for you in regard to the concern that brought you in.
- How did that happen?
- What did you do differently?
- What's different about those times?
- What's different about the times when you're able to get more of an upper hand with the problem?
- What persons, places, or things were helpful to you?
- How will you know when things are better?
- What will be different in your life?
- What have others failed to notice about the problem/situation that brought you here?

Again, notice that these questions are subtle and don't ask for extreme differences. We don't ask, "When is your life problem-free?" That is too big a leap for most and can prove invalidating for those who may get the sense that RYCWs are glossing over problems, moving too quickly, or perhaps focusing too extensively on solutions. It is important to let youth and those involved know that YCWs understand their pain and not give short shrift to their concerns. Using questions that elicit small

Making Contact 53

differences can do this and can be enough to help move in the direction of positive change.

Personal Characteristics/Qualities

- What qualities do you have that you seem to be able to tap into in times of trouble?
- What is it about you that allows to you to keep going?
- What is it about you that seems to come to the forefront when you're facing difficult situations/problems?
- What is it about you that lets you keep going despite all that you've faced?
- Who are you that you've been able to face up to the challenges that life has presented you?
- What would others say are the qualities you have that keep you going?
- What have the qualities that you have allowed you to do that you might not have otherwise done?
- Given the type of person that you are, what do you do on a regular basis to manage the challenges that you face?
- How have you managed, in the midst of all that's happened, to keep going? How have you done that?
- Tell me about a time when you were able to deal with something that could have stopped you from moving forward in life. What did you do?

Culture/Ethnicity/Religion or Spirituality

- How do you identify yourself culturally?
- How does your culture influence your everyday life?
- In what ways, in any, does your nationality influence your everyday life?
- What does spirituality or religion or higher power mean to you?
- How do you experience spirituality or religion or higher power?
- What is most meaningful to you about your [culture, ethnic background, nationality, spiritual beliefs, etc.]?
- How has your [culture, ethnic background, nationality, spiritual beliefs, etc.] been a resource for you?
- How do you maintain its presence in your life?

Family/Social Relationships

- Who are you closest to in your [group, life, family, etc.]?
- What do you appreciate most about your relationship with _____?

54   *Making Contact*

- What would he/she/they say are your best qualities as a [friend, father/mother, caregiver, uncle/aunt, grandparent, peer, etc.]?
- How is it helpful for you to know that?
- What does it feel like to know that?
- Which relationships have been more challenging/difficult for you?
- How have you dealt with those challenges/difficulties?
- Whom can you go to for help?
- Who has made a positive difference in your life?
- How so?
- What difference has that made for you?
- When are others most helpful to you?

Education/School

- How did you manage to make it to/through [a specific grade, middle school, high school, trade school, two years of college, etc.]?
- What qualities do you possess that made that happen?
- What did you like best about school?
- What did you find most challenging/difficult about school?
- How did you manage any difficulties that you may have encountered while in school? [e.g., completing homework/assignments, tests, getting to school on time, moving from one grade to another, teacher/classmate relationships, sports, etc.]
- In what ways did school prepare you for future challenges?

Work/Employment (if applicable)

- How did you get your current job?
- How did you get yourself into position to get the job?
- What do you think your employer saw in you that might have contributed to your being hired?
- What have you found to be most challenging or difficult about your job?
- How have you met or worked toward meeting those challenges/difficulties?
- What keeps you there?
- What skills or qualities do you think your employer sees in you?
- What qualities do you think you possess that are assets on the job?
- [If unemployed] What kind of employment would you like to see yourself involved with in the future?
- What would be a first step for you in making that happen?

Hobbies/Interests

- What do you do for fun?
- What hobbies or interests do you have or have you had in the past?

Making Contact   55

- What kinds of activities are you drawn to?
- What kinds of activities would you rather not be involved with?
- What would you rather do instead?

Previous Placement (Service) Experiences

- What did you find helpful about previous services?
- What did the RYCW or other staff person do that was helpful?
- How did that make a difference for you?
- What wasn't so helpful?
- How have you managed to keep going in placement?
- [If currently or previously on psychotropic medication] How is/was the medication helpful to you?
- What, if anything, did/does the medication allow you to do that you wouldn't otherwise be or have been able to do?
- What qualities do you possess so that you were/are able to work with the medication to improve things for yourself?

These questions are a starting point. In fact, what effective RYCWs tend to do is develop their own questions based on the types on information-gathering processes required of their setting. Our aim is to engage youth and supportive others—collaborate around concerns and ways to address those concerns to the benefit of those most affected. And although information gathering or assessment begins with initial contacts, we still want to continue with strengths-based questions until goals and outcomes are met and there is a measurable benefit of residential services.

A final thought about information gathering relates to the 80/20 rule, which states that 80% of the results or value comes from 20% of the source or focus. The suggestion is that of all the information gathering by RYCWs (and all residential staff), only a small percentage is actually useful in helping youth in residential programs. Our aim then is to streamline our intake and assessment process so that the information we are gathering is actually useful and not a waste of time to youth, supportive others, *and* RYCWs. This idea is discussed at length in relation to YFS elsewhere (see Bertolino, 2014).

Gain Focus: Develop a Vision of the Purpose of Services

A final aspect of initial information gathering and assessment is to gain focus—a clear vision of the purpose of services. The purpose depends on the reason a youth is in a residential program to begin with. There are two very general categories when it comes to youth who are in residential placements. The first category includes youth who are homeless, have been removed from their homes due to some form of abuse or trauma, or have committed serious offenses. In these cases the purpose of services is

56 *Making Contact*

to help youth transition to a setting (e.g., foster home, other residential placement, independent living) other than home. Youth in this category have more often than not been placed by child welfare or protective services, the courts, or other forms of law enforcement.

A second category is comprised of youth who are placed "privately," by their caregivers, usually their legal guardians (i.e., individuals, not systems). A distinction between the first and second categories is more often than not for youth to return home. In such cases the purpose of services varies depending on the original reason for placement. And even though many youth are placed residentially for a family time-out, the reason for the time-out can substantially differ. For example, some youth have trouble with status offenses (i.e., running away, truancy, curfew violation, minor alcohol possession, etc.), others may have school problems (other than truancy), and still others may have trouble with family conflict.

With all youth in residential programs, there is an overall purpose of providing a safe, structured experience in which all their needs are met. Beyond this overarching goal, we want to get more specific regarding the "secondary" purpose of service. To do this we collaborate with youth, caregivers, and others who have the ability to initiate or end services about what they believe needs to happen for services to be deemed effective or beneficial. We refer to these unique purposes as "achievable goals," which are brought about by the actions of youth and supportive others. Identification of achievable goals directs us toward the question: *How will we know when it's better?* There are two characteristics of achievable goals; they are 1) collaborative and agreed upon by all parties involved; and, 2) defined in clear, descriptive terms.

Collaborative Goals

Beyond safe environments in which youth get their needs met are more specific goals that are unique and individualized. We want to know what will indicate that a placement has been helpful. We ask questions such as these:

- What are you hoping will be different as a result of [name of youth] being part of our program?
- Let's say that this placement has been helpful in getting things back on track—how will you know?
- At the end of services, what will [name of youth] be doing that will indicate that things are sufficiently better?
- When you feel [name of youth] has turned the corner and is doing better, what will he or she be doing differently? What difference will that make?

With caregivers or those who have the authority to make future service determinations (i.e., begin or end services, place a youth elsewhere), it can be helpful to suggest examples of change. One possibility is to

Making Contact 57

offer multiple choice questions such as, "Will she be doing _____ or _____ or _____?" The person(s) can then select one of the choices offered or come up with a different description altogether.

To understand what youth and others want to be different, it is necessary to clarify both what difference looks like and how we can provide services that contribute to those clear descriptions. In the next section, we will explore a key process for creating collaborative goals.

Clear and Descriptive: Action-Talk

One of the ways to strengthen our residential programs and further define the role of RYCWs is by clarifying both problems and goals—what we are trying to collectively achieve through services. To help clarify we turn to *action-talk*, which involves translating vague, nonsensory-based words and phrases (e.g., "He's a troublemaker," "She's out of control," "He has ADD," etc.) into clear, objective, observable, and measurable terms. For example, if a parent claims that his son has a "bad attitude," the RYCW inquires as to how his son *expresses* a bad attitude. That is, what does he *do* that signals to the parent that a bad attitude is present?

Below is an example of how a RYCW can use action-based language to obtain a clear description of the concern:

PARENT: My worst fear is that Lisa will continue to act out at school and eventually get expelled. I'm very frustrated.

RYCW: I can hear your frustration. And so that I don't contribute to your frustration, let me make sure I understand. When you say that Lisa has continued to act out in school, what specifically has she done that is most concerning?

PARENT: Well, she gets up and walks around the room and interferes with other students who are trying to do their work.

RYCW: I see. So sometimes she gets up out of her chair and walks around the room. How does she interfere with other students? What does she do?

PARENT: She waves her hands in front of their faces and tries to distract them or she stands in front of them and calls them names.

In addition to a problem description, RYCWs want to gain a goal description. We continue with the previous example to learn how to use action-talk to determine what will indicate positive change:

RYCW: If we were to leap forward to a point in the future in which Lisa was doing better in school and the concern that led her to come to our program for a time-out were resolved, what would be different?

PARENT: Lisa wouldn't be wandering around the room at school and distracting other kids. Then neither of us would be so stressed about school.

58   *Making Contact*

RYCW: What would Lisa be doing instead of walking around the room and disturbing other students?

PARENT: Well, she would sit and do her work.

RYCW: Okay, Lisa would sit and do her work. And I will ask Lisa this as well—what would you experience instead of stress?

PARENT: I would feel calm and relaxed.

RYCW: So if I saw you walking down the street and you were calm and relaxed, how would I know?

PARENT: I would be smiling, maybe talking to a friend, laughing . . .

Because youth and supportive others will often describe what they don't want, we make sure to inquire as to what needs to happen *instead*. This keeps services future focused. In addition, we continue conversations to achieve goals that are realistic and solvable. Finally, a creative way of using action-talk is *video-talk*. This method involves having youth and/other others describe both problems and solutions as if they can be seen on video. Continuing with the recent example, here is how video-talk might be used:

> If you were to video record Lisa in school and the problem that brought you here was happening and I were to watch that video, what would I see? What specifically would she be doing that would indicate to me that she was out of control?

Although action-talk is a method, it is also a process that RYCWs can use in virtually all aspects of YFS. This is because we often speak in ambiguities and generalizations, the result of which can be misunderstanding and misguided attempts to help. Action-talk helps us gain clarity about problems or concerns as well as what "better" might look like. And this second part is particularly important because we are developing a clear purpose of services. Video-talk is a creative way of using action. There are also other creative ways of working with youth and their support networks to develop a vision of the purpose of services. Next are a few of these examples.

The Miracle Question

This popular method can be used to help youth and supportive others envision futures in which their problems have been solved (de Shazer, 1988). The miracle question is, "Suppose you were to go home tonight, and while you were asleep, a miracle happened and this problem was solved. How will you know the miracle happened? What will be different?" (p. 5). This question is followed up in detail with questions about the miracle scenario given.

The Dream Method

A variation of the miracle question is the dream method (Bertolino, 2003). The RYCW asks, "Let's suppose that tonight, while you are sleeping, you have a dream. In this dream the problem you have is resolved. Tell me about what might happen in that dream that would lead to your problem no longer being a problem. What might happen?" Another variation is to speculate about a past dream: "Suppose that you had a wonderful dream last night or sometime in the recent past. Up until now, however, you haven't been able to recall it. In that dream, you were able to see your future without the problem that brought you to me. What happened?" As with other methods described in this section, the youth and/or other's response is further developed through follow-up questions.

The Time Machine

Another way of gaining a sense of the purpose of services that can be particularly useful with youth is the time machine (Bertolino, 1999). It is a way to help them to envision a future where things work out. The time machine is introduced in the following way:

> Let's say there is a time machine sitting here in the office. Let's say that you climb in and it propels you into the future, to a time when things are going the way you want them to go. After arriving at your future destination, the first thing you notice is that the problems that brought you to therapy have disappeared.

Next the RYCW helps youth to develop the scenario with questions such as these:

- Where are you?
- Who is with you?
- What is happening?
- What are you doing?
- How is your life different than before?
- Where did your problems go?
- How did they go away?

Picture It

Two final variations here are to have a youth visualize seeing his or her future as if it were a movie playing on a screen (Bertolino, Kiener, & Patterson, 2009) or to imagine using a View-Master (a child's toy similar to binoculars in which images are on a small reel and can be changed by clicking a switch; see Bertolino, 1999). By now you understand the concept of helping youth envision futures in which their lives are going better—in which problems are more manageable, if not absent altogether.

For some youth physical props (such as pictures or drawings) will help with developing a future focus. For example, a youth could be asked to create an image on paper of the future she would like by drawing a

60   *Making Contact*

picture or using cutouts from magazines. The idea is to use what fits for the youth. Whether using basic questions or creative methods, RYCWs want to help youth gain clarity and answer the rudimentary question, "How will you know when things are better?" Once what youth or others involved want is clear, practitioners can begin to collaborate with them on steps to make those positive changes occur.

Signposts

There is one remaining and often understated area related to gaining focus regarding the purpose of services. Through face-to-face initial contacts, we learn what problems/concerns look like and what will indicate improvement. And yet there are times that youth and others will see the gap between the two as rather large and insurmountable. And when youth and supportive others do not feel that progress is being made, frustration, loss of hope, and increased problems result. Even worse, this puts youth at greater risk of both giving up and dropping out of services.

To better understand this point, let's return once more to a theme of the last chapter: what Walt Disney knew, or, more accurately, what the Walt Disney Company collectively knows. Estimates are that the capacity of Disneyland is between 75,000 and 85,000 patrons. Now combine that many people and long lines to get on rides and have a meal with a very hot summer day in Anaheim, California. What do you get? A great deal of frustration, irritability, and inevitably anger. At those times Disneyland is *not a happy place*. The result is that some give up and leave—but not without first complaining.

So what has Disney done? Well, quite a lot, actually, although much of it is subtle. Given that many complaints relate to the attractions (e.g., long lines, broken rides), theme park operators have become resourceful and ingenious in coming up with ways of keeping people happy. One strategy Disney has used is to begin the entertainment as soon as patrons are in line. There are television monitors showing videos, music piped in, things to look at and read while in line, and oftentimes refreshments within reach. A second strategy Disney has utilized involves multitiered rides. A ride, for example, may begin with people standing in a room viewing a video or with a park attendant who tells a story, followed by a guided walk through a second part, and may end with the people getting on the ride itself. The point is this: Park visitors are entertained throughout the attraction even though the lines to get on "rides" are often long. A third strategy is the "Fast Pass." Originally offered for an additional fee (which other parks still charge a premium fee for), it is now available to all park visitors at no additional cost. The most recent version, The Fast Past+, allows patrons to make reservations in advance for park attractions. And while there are restrictions to the Fast Pass process (i.e., patrons can only Fast Pass a limited number of attractions per day, some

Making Contact 61

attractions cannot be Fast-Passed, time slots are first-come-first-served), benefits such as having a schedule (a major bonus for families with young children in particular) and shorter wait times for chosen attractions are invaluable. The result? Less frustration and greater joy for park goers.

Why do these strategies matter? Because frustration is problematic. Of course frustration at a theme park is very different and far less serious compared to a youth who experiences frustration in a residential setting. In residential services, when youth or others involved (especially those who have the ability to begin and end services) get the sense that they are not making progress, they are at higher risk of not just giving up, but for prematurely ending services.

And yet what we can do to neutralize or even prevent frustration in YFS mirrors what happens at Disney. Disney knows that when people are engaged (through entertainment, in its case), with the sense that they are moving and making progress toward their destinations—getting on the ride—they are less likely to become irritated, frustrated, or angry; drop out of line; and perhaps leave the park. As RYCWs we can orient youth to what can happen *between* the problem and the vision of an improved future. We do this through identifying indicators or signposts that progress is being made toward the established goals. Here are some questions to assist with the identification of signposts or movement toward goals:

- What will be the first sign or indication that things have begun to turn the corner with your problem?
- What will be the first sign or indication to you that you have taken a solid step on the road to improvement even though you might not yet be out of the woods?
- What's one thing that might indicate to you that things are on the upswing?
- What will you see happening when things are beginning to go more the way you'd like them to go?
- What would have to happen that would indicate to you that things are changing in the direction you'd like them to change?
- How will you know when the change you are looking for has started?
- What is happening right now with your situation that you would like to have continue?

Action-talk remains an integral process of conversation about signposts to progress. We want to help youth and others identify what specifically will be different, including how those things happen, when they happen, who is involved, and so on. We aren't seeking explanations, rather the "4WHs"—the who, what, when, where, and how—of the progress.

By focusing on movement—how we will know we are making progress—RYCWs can help youth realize their gains and how those gains

62   *Making Contact*

relate to their overall idea of what constitutes improvement. Doing so can also counter the frustration that youth and others experience, help with the acquisition of new skills, increase hope, and increase motivation to "stay the course."

Future Considerations: Becoming Outcome Driven

The fourth strengths-based principle is: "Effective services promote growth, development, and well-being." Thus far we have explored the overall purpose (i.e., safe environment in which needs are met, preparation for transition to another setting, etc.) of residential services and goals that are unique to each youth and his or her support system. But there is a remaining thread—well-being—without which the effectiveness of residential services cannot be appropriately evaluated. As described in the strength-based definition, well-being is a construct comprised of three areas of functioning: individual, interpersonal relationships, and social role. Collectively, these three elements translate to outcome. In other words, improved well-being equals improved outcome.

So how do we measure outcome? Let's return to the last line in the strengths-based definition: "Routine and ongoing real-time feedback is used to maintain a responsive, consumer-driven climate to ensure the greatest benefit of services." Real-time feedback is comprised of two forms of measurement—*outcome* and *alliance*. *Outcome* measurement refers to the idiosyncratic meaning youth and supportive others attach to services. To do this we elicit youth and supportive others' reports of the subjective benefit of services at the *beginning* of meetings (or sessions or interactions). Through ongoing monitoring of outcomes, RYCWs are able to learn whether and to what degree services provided are beneficial and make adjustments accordingly.

Alliance measurement involves monitoring the four components of the alliance described in Chapter 1: the client's view of the relationship (including perceptions of the provider as warm, empathic, and genuine); agreement on the goals, meaning, or purpose of the treatment; agreement on the means and methods used; and the client's preferences. Formal alliance measurement takes place at the *end* of each meeting (or session or interaction) to learn how the youth and/or supportive other experienced the interaction. However, alliance monitoring also involves periodically checking in. We want answers to these questions: Are youth feeling heard and understood? Are they satisfied with the direction of services? Do they feel the means used to achieve goals are a good fit? As meetings/sessions/interactions progress and end, RYCWs and/or other YFS staff check with youth to learn their perceptions of interactions—again learning what worked well, what did not—and make any necessary adjustments to accommodate their preferences.

Routine in the context of residential programs means on average measuring both outcome and alliance once a week. If more than a week passes without monitoring change, there is a greater likelihood that a youth will improve or deteriorate without residential staff noticing. Warren, Nelson, Burlingame, and Mondragon (2012) found that failure to monitor progress on a routine basis (ideally meeting by meeting/session by session) to identify those at risk of deterioration in youth services led to substantially more cases of negative outcome. Conversely, ongoing and routine measurement reduced the rate of service failure. In residential services, more frequent measurement is not likely to allow enough time to pass to see change occur; therefore, the aim is to find a balance in terms of when and how often to use measurement.

The importance of outcome measurement cannot be understated. Whether the form of service is outpatient or outclient therapy, residential treatment, or another form, change begins early in services (Miller, Duncan, & Hubble, 1997). And when youth experience meaningful change early in services, the probability of a measurable positive outcome significantly increases (Haas et al., 2002; Percevic et al., 2006; Whipple et al., 2003). Conversely, when youth show little or no improvement or experience a worsening of symptoms early in services, they are at higher risk for negative outcome—a worsening of problems, dropout, and so on (Bertolino et al., 2013; Duncan et al., 2010). In residential programs, lack of benefit early in services is likely to contribute to greater frustration and loss faith in services, for both youth *and* all staff. The evidence therefore suggests a focus on tracking the benefit of services from the start of services.

There are numerous measurement tools available for both monitoring outcome and alliance. There are benefits and drawbacks to each such as length, cost, and so forth. For those interested in a more detailed account, I have discussed how to implement outcome measurement in the book *Thriving on the Front Lines: A Guide to Strengths-Based Youth Care Work* (Bertolino, 2014). The point is for RYCWs to take interest in whether or not their relationships are a good fit for youth and to what degree services are of benefit.

Thoughts on Level Systems

A common facet among residential programs is level systems. The tradition of level systems in residential programs is long, due in large part to an emphasis on behavioral strategies. There are standard frameworks that are based on performance of tasks, completion of required activities, adherence to rules, and so on. Level systems are a standard and are neither good nor bad. They are a tool that can be effective in helping youth grow and change or they can be used punitively as a means of punishment. A general benefit of level systems is that they provide a consistent

64 *Making Contact*

means of providing rewards and consequences, versus punishment, along a continuum of program expectations. Level systems also provide a single framework that is easily understood by both program staff and youth.

A primary idea of level systems is for youth to achieve "promotions" to higher levels. For example, a youth may be promoted a level or two—usually meaning she attains more privileges and perhaps independence—based on completion of program goals and responsible behavior. Oftentimes there is a process youth must go through to be promoted, such as completing "level assignments" and/or being interviewed by a RYCW, for example. Table 3.1 provides an example of a form that can be used for level promotions.

Youth can also receive level "drops," which are a form of consequence for violating the rules of a program. In such case a youth may fall a level or two. These may be short-term drops that are time contingent, meaning that youth will return to their previous level after a set amount of time. Alternatively, youth may be required to re-petition for a level promotion. Depending on the program philosophy, level changes can be made by persons on a given shift or can be team decisions. For example, in some programs decisions about level promotions are made in weekly staffings, which will be discussed in the next chapter. And although it is a fading practice, level systems are in some cases still used as a way to determine whether or not a youth is ready to "graduate" or transition out of a program (Durrant, 1993).

A concern with level systems is the implication that change is a one-way street. There is the prevailing assumption that youth who are truly making progress will do so linearly, in a positive, upward fashion. In actuality, youth most often move back and forth—forward and backward—when it comes to lasting change (Prochaska & DiClemente, 2005). Durrant (1993) points out that even though level systems appear to be based on rewarding successful behavior, they may easily contribute to ideas of failure. Setbacks that are often part of learning may carry purely negative connotations, even though they may just be part of a youth's growing. For youth who have histories of difficulties that have contributed to a sense of failure, this feeling may be reinforced by doing poorly within a framework of a level system.

One additional concern with level systems: For some youth, the goal may become to attain a higher level when achieving that level should be just a part of a more successful future. Although residential programs rely on structure, and level systems assist with structure, it is crucial that RYCWs understand that level promotions are but one indicator of progress. As discussed earlier, there are far more robust indicators of improvement—starting with outcomes based on real-time feedback.

From a collaborative, strengths-based perspective, our aim is to foster positive change by identifying and leveraging the strengths of youth. Therefore, level systems are opportunities to build capacity and ability.

Table 3.1 Form With Strengths-Based Language to Use for Level Petitions and Promotions

Level Promotion Petition Form

Name: _____ Date: _____

Current Level: _____ Level Petitioning for: _____

Interviewed by: _____

Describe three of your strengths (things you believe you do well, things you are good at, or things that help you deal with challenges and hard times).

1.

2.

3.

Describe something you have become better at while in this program. If you can think of a second thing, describe that one too.

1.

2.

List a goal that you set for yourself while in this program. Then, describe what you have done to work toward achieving that goal.

Goal: _____

What I have done to work toward my goal: _____

_____

Write down anything you think staff should consider in reviewing your petition for a level promotion.

_____

Signature of Youth

66 *Making Contact*

Let's consider some questions that RYCWs can incorporate when making decisions about level changes:

- What kinds of things have you done over the past [time frame] to move you toward the goals you have set for yourself here?
- What are you doing to keep yourself heading in a direction that will help you be where you want, or at least a few steps closer to where you want, once you leave here?
- How did you manage to complete [number of] tasks today?
- [If using a point system] What did you do to earn [number of] points today?
- What will you do to continue being successful over the next few days?
- What have you done or what will you be doing to show staff, as a whole, that you are ready for more responsibility?
- What do you think shows that you are ready to be promoted to the next level?
- What will you do if you have a little slipup? How will you keep things from getting worse?

These examples can be modified or added to depending on the program. Our focus is to draw on strengths, to evoke ability and help youth grow over time. We expect youth to stumble, and then get up, and then stumble again. And over time, with our support, their footing becomes more firm, as do their decisions. This process will help youth build confidence. Level systems are a tool to help youth, not hinder them.

In settings in which forms are used when youth petition for higher levels, there are opportunities to use strengths-based language. Table 3.1 offers an example of one such form. It is important that when staff use level petition forms, they spend time talking with youth about the meaning of their responses. Action-talk is also a necessary vehicle for clarifying any vague descriptions or statements of youth. In the event that a level promotion is not granted, RYCWs give clear feedback about what youth are expected to do that will serve as evidence for their next petition and a time frame as to when they are eligible to apply again. This will provide encouragement and hope.

4 We're in This Together
Teaming Up for Change

Most residential facilities rely on a *team approach*. Teams can include social workers, counselors, therapists, case managers, psychologists, psychiatrists, primary care physicians, nurses, nutritionists, recreation therapists, music therapists, art therapists, treatment coordinators, and, most importantly, RYCWs. Many such staff also serve as directors, managers, or supervisors. Some programs are more lean, staff-wise, than others. For example, unless a program strictly serves youth with substance abuse issues or is affiliated with a hospital, that program is unlikely to have a full-time physician. The same is often the case when it comes to specialized staff such as nutritionists and recreational therapists. Furthermore, some short-terms programs do not provide "therapy" per se. Instead they rely primarily on skilled staff to provide services such as crisis management and case management.

A unique characteristic of YFS teams is the diverse educational and training backgrounds of those who make up the teams. This is because psychiatrists are trained differently than psychologists, who are trained differently than counselors, who are trained differently than social workers, and so on. And when we add in RYCWs, who also differ in terms of education and training, there is both a greater risk of competing ideologies and a greater chance of opportunities to draw on the diverse perspectives represented in residential services.

As we know, although most residential programs have staff with well-defined roles, there is also the necessity of wearing multiple "hats." The expectation is that staff will contribute when needed. An analogy might be what is referred to as "bullpen by committee" in baseball. In the biggest games—the kind that determine whether or not a team will advance—any player could be called on to enter the game and do what is asked of him.

But a fact is that many of the everyday tasks in residential programs will be the responsibility of RYCWs, who by virtue of their role are arguably the most integral cogs in the wheel of services. They keep programs running. So, by role, RYCWs will also be the most versatile staff—doing whatever it takes for their programs.

68   *We're in This Together*

So how do RYCWs function as part of larger residential teams? What is their role? In this chapter we will explore these and other questions regarding the role of RYCWs on teams and how to incorporate collaborative, strengths-based strategies to open up possibilities for working with youth.

All Together Now: RYCWs and Effective Teamwork

In the companion book to this one, *Thriving on the Front Lines: A Guide to Strengths-Based Youth Care Work*, I offer several guiding ideas followed by a series of structural guidelines for teams in YFS (Bertolino, 2014). A brief summary of each is provided here. We begin with the three guiding ideas.

Guiding Ideas for Residential Teams

1. *Have confidence in yourself and your team members.* Because RYCWs have enormous responsibility, decisiveness is a necessity. And decisiveness requires confidence. Being confident does not mean having all the answers. Instead it means an unwavering belief that we are capable of maintaining a safe climate and getting the job done. We must have confidence in our abilities, our colleagues, our services, and our institutions. Conversely, overconfident teams make mistakes because they tend to lack balance between intuition and training. Effective teams involve team members' personal insights and evidence—with checks and balances to ensure consistency in both decisions and actions.
2. *Expect the best but be prepared for the worst.* RYCWs are the glue that holds things together. RYCWs strive to balance optimism with realism, remaining on the lookout for exceptions and successes while keeping a finger on the pulse of potential areas of concern. RYCWs "glance at problems, gaze at strengths," using strengths-based language and interventions to facilitate present and future change. Preparation involves preparing for the worst, which *is* strengths based. This is because preparation requires using our abilities to deal with whatever comes our way. And the most effective preparatory practice is that which involves real-life situations. Rather than making up hypothetical situations, it is more effective to use situations that have happened. Then teams can pool their ideas to explore potential courses of action. RYCWs must be at the center of such discussions rather than being told what to do and how to do it. Differences have to be worked out within teams or those differences will lead to larger, perhaps more serious concerns around safety. Teams that are on the same page provide more consistent and reliably effective services.
3. *Work together.* RYCWs have to communicate openly and clearly with one another—knowing when to step in for the other, when to defer to another, and so on. Effective teams are reliant on team members knowing their roles and responsibilities and being flexible enough to

step out of those roles when situations arise. There can be competitions for heroism—our success lies in the ability to work collectively without losing focus on the tasks at hand.

Before delving into more specific things RYCWs can do as part of teams, let's consider some structural guidelines to import directly into conversations, meetings, and overall decision-making processes.

The Sum Is Greater

In *Thriving on the Front Lines*, I told the story of Francis Galton, a cousin to Charles Darwin, and an ox-weighing contest. In the contest, for a small fee, participants could guess the weight of an ox, with the person guessing closest winning the ox. Galton saw the competition as an opportunity to do an experiment. He assumed that the crowd, made up largely of those who had little expertise in livestock, would have poor judging capabilities and thereby have no chance of calculating the weight of the ox. But Galton was wrong. When he calculated the mean of the guesses from those who placed a wager, he was shocked to discover that the average guess of the crowd was 1,197 pounds, just one pound less than the actual weight of the ox. The crowd's judgment was right on. Galton later wrote about his finding: "The result seems more credible to the trustworthiness of a democratic judgment than might have been expected" (Bertolino, 2014, p. 452).

Residential teams include people with varying backgrounds and degrees of experience. But no matter how smart the individual members, the collective intelligence of the group is a far greater resource. Even when groups are comprised of members with less individual knowledge or those who are not especially well-informed, they can still reach collectively wise decisions. This idea has been referred to as "the wisdom of crowds" (Surowiecki, 2004).

Residential teams can work more effectively by following a few simple structural guidelines. First is to encourage diversity of opinion. Each member of a team should have his or her own point of view, even if it's just an interpretation of the known facts. Teams who are able to explore differing points of view generate more, and a wider range of, possibilities for action than those that tend to be homogenous. A second structural guideline is to value independence. The process of arriving at a collective decision should not be through coercion, force, or subversion. Instead, collective decisions result from each team member having the freedom to convey his or her thoughts and ideas in a supportive context.

Third is to decentralize to strengthen. Some team members will specialize and/or have specific roles and responsibilities based on their local knowledge, which continues to evolve over time through experience, practice, and relationships. Differing roles can benefit collective decision making and what happens when putting those decisions into action. A

70 We're in This Together

fourth and final structural point is for teams to move toward aggregation. Doing so involves having some mechanism for turning private judgments into collective decisions. The process of moving from multiple sometimes disparate viewpoints is part of the structure implemented from the start. There is a rationale and method in place to move conversations toward collective decisions. Residential teams are most successful when decisions are arrived at not by team members modifying their positions or through compromise but when teams embrace and encourage diversity and independence and figure out how to use mechanisms that support the collective group as a whole.

RYCWs in Action: Stepping Forward on Teams

There is a scene in the 1998 film *The Horse Whisperer* in which two of the main characters have a conversation about life. One of the characters, Tom, played by Robert Redford, describes how a relationship came to an end. He says, "It wasn't meant to be." To this, Annie, played by Kristin Scott Thomas, asks, "But how did you know, for sure?" Tom replies, "Knowing is the easy part. Saying it out loud is the hard part." Many RYCWs can relate to Tom's statement. This is because there are many times that something occurs, during a staffing, for example, and the RYCW feels strongly about what's happening. There is a strong gut feeling, and yet the RYCW does not speak up. The thing is, when we say something out loud, two things occur. The first is that once it's been said, it's out there. Others have heard the point of view of the person who said it. The second is that once something is said, there is the expectation of action. Both the sharing of views and taking action are crucial to the success of teams.

When it comes to RYCWs taking more of a leadership role with teams, there is little gray area. Youth cannot afford for us to be passive in meetings. They need us to step forward, be as assertive as necessary, stand up for them, and take action. Perhaps the most common avenue for RYCWs to step forward is in team meetings, or *staffings* as they as sometimes known, which will be discussed next.

Opportunities Abound: Team Meetings, Staffings, and Case Conferences

In most residential settings, teams meet regularly to discuss the needs of youth, set up service plans to meet those needs, and coordinate activities for youth and supportive others (Krueger, 1990). Team meetings, staffings, or case conferences, as they are sometimes called, typically occur once a week with most if not all program staff required to attend. Here we will use the term "staffings" to refer to *opportunities* for staff present to offer feedback about challenges and successes and potential hurdles to future success both with youth and with programs as a whole. They can also be used to train in new skills and/or convey information to staff as a whole. For example, some residential programs conduct in-services to meet licensing or funding requirements.

The overall purpose of staffings is to ensure that youth are receiving the highest quality of care. To do this ongoing evaluation of what is and is not working is essential. Despite serving as forums for promoting change, team meetings do not always go as planned and can take on a negative tone. One of the ways these meetings turn negative is when a staff person engages in pathology-based conversation (see Chapter 2), often by using "problem-talk," labeling a youth or a youth's behavior in pathological terms. Some comments are casual and end after they are spoken. Yet a negative statement can lead to another and then another. I see negative comments as the result of staff not seriously considering the ramifications of their statements or points of view. Unfortunately it only takes a time or two for there to be a domino effect. Once a negative thread begins, it can swell into conversation about all that is perceived to be wrong with a youth. Without someone stepping in, pathology-based conversations can rapidly snowball as more staff join in. I refer to these kinds of rapidly progressing negative conversations as "staff infections," which can have disastrous consequences when it comes to the quality of services, staff satisfaction, and the like (Bertolino, 2011).

To better understand the point of negativity in staffings, we make a distinction between talking about problems and pathology-based conversations. A focus of staffings is to be clear on what is happening with youth that is of concern. We can use action-talk to describe behaviors in clear and concise ways and identify goals through the same process. We can also talk about how some behaviors are more challenging than others. So, we are not problem-phobic. We simply want to have respectful, constructive conversations.

In contrast, pathology-based conversations such as those outlined in Chapter 2 do little other than upset people. They do not help with clarifying problems, they are not respectful, they do not help staff know what to do differently. Instead, pathology-based conversations in staffings allow staff to pile on a bandwagon of negativity that frequently leads to discussions about how to get youth out of programs rather than about what can be done to help youth be successful.

Not long after I was hired as a RYCW, I found myself struggling in our regular staffings. My experience was that we would be having a productive conversation about a youth, and then, seemingly out of nowhere, a shift would occur. The shift was in the form of a comment, such as, "Kayla can be a real troublemaker." From there other RYCWs might pile on, and the landslide would begin. The illusion was that negativity appeared spontaneously and out of the blue. But I soon came to understand that negativity was the result of three very specific things.

The first relates to personal philosophy. As discussed in Chapter 1, there is no way around the fact that one's core beliefs will eventually surface.

72 We're in This Together

Working with youth is stressful. Exploring core beliefs and assumptions about youth and factors such as how change occurs is important to knowing one's self more thoroughly. When staff respond negatively in staff meetings, sometimes they just haven't thought things through and have failed to evaluate the consequences of their personal belief systems.

A second reason negativity can develop a life of its own in staffings is because staff have not learned how to use language as a vehicle for change. To remedy this we practice how to identify pathology-based conversations and problem-talk and ways to engage in strengths-based conversations and solution-talk.

Third, and perhaps the one source of negativity most likely to fly under the radar, is when RYCWs or staff who spend substantial time with youth and each other let something linger. Sometimes things lay dormant until someone feels invalidated or unsupported, and then a sore spot flares up. For instance, a RYCW might have a point of view that is unintentionally but nonetheless dismissed by another person during a staffing. Feeling invalidated, the RYCW becomes defensive and either speaks negatively or closes down to others.

So what can RYCWs do in staffings to respond to the aforementioned sources of negativity as well as other not mentioned? Let's first consider how we can move staffings *toward* achievable ends such as better services, improved staff cohesion, increased well-being among staff, and so forth. In other words, how can we turn negativity into opportunity? In the sections that follow, we explore several ways to do this.

Diffuse Negativity Through Acknowledgment and Possibility

A theme so far through this book has been to keep things simple. In far too many cases, trying to get fancy by making situations more complex only further complicates matters. All the methods described in this book can be applied not only to situations with youth but also with staff. And an excellent place to stimulate change is by building relationships though listening and attending.

In the previous chapter, we learned about various ways to engage through attending. One of the methods described involves the use of acknowledgment and possibility. Just as we would do with youth and supportive others, we use language to acknowledge the differing perspectives that are present at staffings and inject the element of possibility. To do this, we listen carefully to each staff person's viewpoint and then begin to paint doorways in corners with our words. Here is an example:

RYCW 1: He [the youth] is always arguing with me about what he's supposed to be doing. He's not getting any better with directions.

RYCW 2: He's argued with you a lot, and it seems to you like he hasn't got any better with directions.

We're in This Together 73

In this example, RYCW 2 acknowledged RYCW 1's perspective while also adding the element of possibility by using the past tense ("argued"), translating into a partial statement ("a lot"), and translating into a perception ("it seems to you"). Being a RYCW is a role, and because we are all human beings, we will not always respond well if we feel invalidated. So a first step is to listen. And as we listen, we can acknowledge and seek opportunities to open up closed-down statements. We do not always have to agree with what has been said, but we should make every attempt to understand each other's point of view. If we expect someone to consider our perspective, we need to acknowledge theirs. So by focusing on language, we can gradually change the tone of staffings.

Bring It to the Table: The Qualities of RYCWs

Each person has something to contribute to a staffing. What are your contributions—your assets? If you are unsure, make a list of what you "bring to the table"—what you have to offer. You might also ask your supervisor, colleagues, or the youth with whom you work. To further assist you, I have included "The RYCW Strength List" in Table 4.1. Please complete this list to learn more about your personal characteristics and how you might use them in group or team meetings.

Now consider how your assets connect with the role of RYCW. As a guide, please refer to Table 4.2, "Essential Characteristics of YFS Workers," which provides a list of important qualities of not just RYCWs,

Table 4.1 The RYCW Strength List

The RYCW Strength List
1. The abilities, assets, qualities, and strengths I bring to my role and setting that help me to be an effective RYCW: Abilities: Assets: Qualities: Strengths: 2. I can use my abilities, assets, qualities, and strengths to become even better as a RYCW by: 3. I can specifically use my abilities as a member of my residential team by: 4. I have dealt with adversity in the past by: 5. I can use my past experience in dealing with adversity in my job as a RYCW by: 6. I can be present for and support other RYCWs to improve their skills and effectiveness by:

74 *We're in This Together*

Table 4.2 Essential Characteristics of YFS Workers

1. The ability to feel at ease and comfortable with other people, especially young people: Someone who is relaxed and not threatened by personal interaction.
2. The ability to put others, especially young people at ease: Someone others just naturally open up to, quickly.
3. The ability to project unconditional regard and acceptance of others: Someone who is genuinely nonjudgmental or who can appear to be so.
4. The ability to convey warmth and empathy: Someone who projects understanding of others' feelings and thoughts.
5. Good verbal and interpersonal skills: Someone who gets along well in many different situations and with many different kinds of people and who can use language to seem like one of the group.
6. Good listening skills: Someone who pays close attention to what others say and does not feel compelled to always inject personal thoughts and comments into the conversation.
7. The ability to project enthusiasm: Someone who seems genuinely interested in others and whose enthusiasm engages the interest of others.
8. An awareness of one's own nonverbal reactions: Someone who is capable of maintaining body language and facial expressions that project the above traits and does not convey annoyance or frustration.
9. Physical characteristics that are non-threatening, intimidating, or off-putting to others.
10. The ability to *conceptualize* and to think through complex situations as opposed to thinking literally and in a rote manner.

(Brendtro, du Toit, Bath, Bockern, 2006)

but YCWs in general. The same skills RYCWs use on each shift, in every interaction, are also necessary when it comes to teams.

One of the ways teams get bogged down is when staff are unaware of their own assets—what they have to offer to teams. Keep in mind that in doing our own personal survey of abilities, we are paralleling what we do with youth. We search for abilities and then learn how to use more abilities more actively in new and different contexts. Finally, to assist with the development of your abilities, please refer to Table 4.3, the "RYCW Weekly Success Chart."

What You Have to Say Matters: Please, Speak Up

In my first months as a RYCW, there were many times that I sat still, saying nothing. It's not that my mind wasn't churning out ideas. Rather, I questioned my ability and experience compared to others. I wasn't an expert on anything. I didn't think I knew enough to make reasonable assertions. I was afraid to be wrong. So I remained silent.

While I did not think of it this way at the time, my silence was a choice. I chose not to speak up out of fear. But that changed in a moment's time.

We're in This Together   75

Table 4.3 RYCW Weekly Success Chart

RYCW Weekly Success Chart
Name of RYCW:
"Exceptional Work This Week" (Include comments written by the RYCW as well as peers identifying successful actions during the week.)
Goals (Provides what the RYCW wants to accomplish over the course of the next week, or until this form is revised. Goals should be described in specific, behavioral terms [action-talk]. This encourages peers to notice times when the RYCW achieves the goal.)

It was a typical Wednesday staffing, and we were discussing a youth by the name of Trey and how he didn't want to talk about his "anger issues." The conversation frustrated me because I had spent many shifts with Trey. It seemed to me that he had other things on his mind. So when the conversation about his anger persisted, I felt compelled to speak up but was scared to.

And then it all came pouring out, in one fell swoop.

Sometimes I just don't understand . . . If it's me and I was taken away from the ones I love . . . and I had not eaten in a few days . . . and if I had been abused, not to mention whatever else is happening . . . I'm thinking about those things first. If I'm Trey, maybe I'm angry and have every right to be, but that doesn't mean I want to talk about it, and it doesn't mean it's a problem. I can't speak for Trey. I guess I

76 *We're in This Together*

don't understand why we are spending so much time on trying to get Trey to talk about his anger when he has so many other glaring needs like food and safety and a need for compassion? Whose issues are we talking about anyway, his or ours?

I just stared at the table, aware of silence in the room. My face was burning from the rush of blood. And I thought, "I'm going to get fired for this." But I could not sit in silence any longer.

Fortunately one of my colleagues was thinking the same thing. She chimed in. "I think we need to be reminded to stay focused on the residents' needs. If these kids don't have what they need, the rest won't really matter," offered Mary, our lead RYCW. Once Mary spoke, heads nodded in agreement.

Of course I was never in danger of being fired for speaking up. It was just my fear. It was the kind of worry RYCWs sometimes experience. Should I say something? What happens if I do? And so on and so on. So let's put all our self-doubt to rest. What you have to say is as valid as what anyone else has to say.

More importantly, youth need us to speak up. Negativity in staffings can be stopped in its tracks if we show the same sort of courage that youth show every day.

To the Point: Service Planning and Coordination in Staffings

One of the primary points of staffings is service planning, which involves discussing the goals for a youth while in residential treatment. In addition to ensuring that youth have their basic needs met and assessing for risk, we work toward unique and individualized goals. In Chapter 3, in the section, "Gain Focus: Develop a Vision of the Purpose of Services," we learned about how to co-create service goals with youth and supportive others. In cases where a service plan (i.e., treatment plan) requires further clarification or if a service plan has yet to be created, it can be helpful to consider a few overarching questions:

- What led this youth to be placed with us?
- Who placed the youth?
- Who is paying for the placement and/or has the authority to end services?
- How might such persons constrain or affect services or serve as an asset?
- Who is concerned (or complaining or alarmed) the most about the youth?
- What are their concerns? [Be sure to translate vague, nondescriptive, and blaming words into actions descriptions.]
- What would the youth and/or supportive others like to have change or improve as a result of this program?

We're in This Together   77

- What will indicate to the youth and/or supportive others that this program has been successful?
- How will we know that our program has been minimally helpful to this youth?
- What will be a signal that progress, even just a little bit, is occurring with the youth and the situation that led to placement?
- What will be different for the youth and/or supportive others as a result of positive change?
- What strengths, abilities, and resources does the youth and his or her supportive network have that may be helpful with the concerns that led to the youth being placed with us?
- How has the youth and/or supportive others dealt with past adversity or similar difficulties?
- What is currently happening with the youth that might be a step toward improving things just a bit with the youth's situation?
- What can we do as a team to encourage change in a direction that will be most beneficial to this youth?
- What are the legal and ethical restraints or considerations? [i.e., suicidal ideation, intent, or plan; homicidal ideation, intent, or plan; history of violence; outstanding court/legal involvement, etc.]

As always, action-talk helps clarify vague and otherwise ambiguous statements into clear, descriptive ones. The more clear the descriptions, the less chance of misunderstanding there will be and the more focused the attempt to promote change will be. Action-talk also helps ensure that all staff involved share the same focus and are working together. And because service plans are largely carried out by RYCWs, through daily activities, they must be involved in both development and coordination. Next, we always keep the voices of youth front and center when making decisions. To do this while keeping things simple, we use the following guiding ideas in staffing youth:

- Include youth and supportive others in meetings whenever possible.
- If youth cannot be present, invite them to contribute any thoughts or questions they might have.
- Share with youth any points that you would like to make in upcoming meetings, providing rationale and allowing them the opportunity to edit your comments.
- Update youth on the outcome of staffings, case conferences, or meetings, including any ideas or questions that may have been generated.
- Act as if youth are present at meetings to keep conversations respectful and focused.
- Use person-first language and youths' real names, avoiding depersonalizing labels such as "the bipolar kid," "the overreactive grandma," or "the crisis-oriented family" (Bertolino, 2014).

78 We're in This Together

Table 4.4 Who I Am: What I Want Staff to Know About Me

1. What I most want staff to know about me:

2. What some people don't understand about me is:

3. These are the things I want to accomplish while I am here:

4. What I want for myself in the future is:

5. A few things I am good at are:

6. Some things I can get better at are:

7. Staff can help me the most by:

An irony about most residential programs is that many claim to be "youth focused" and yet youth are left out of decisions that directly affect their well-being and future. An example is when youth are left out of staffings. Sometimes youth are not invited because professionals believe they *know* what is going on with youth and what is best for them. Therefore decisions are based on expert decision making without the input of youth. This is an unfortunate and unhelpful assumption.

Being strengths based means going beyond the ideas listed here by scanning for opportunities to both include and highlight the perspectives of youth. That said, it will not always be possible for youth to be physically present at staffings, yet there are alternatives to bring forth their perspective. An example of how to do this is by using questions from Table 4.4, "Who I Am: What I Want Staff to Know About Me." Prior to staffing, youth can be invited to complete the form by saying, "We are having a meeting to talk about how we can best support and help you. Would you mind answering a few questions so that we can be sure to include what you want and think in our conversation?" Youth can then complete all or some of the questions or YCWs can ask questions and write the responses of youth. The form is then shared in staffing as a way to include the view of youth.

The More, the Better? Having Productive Staffings

One of the complaints of not just RYCWs, but all residential staff, relates to the time-benefit equation of staffings. That is, programs often grapple with the issue of how much time to spend discussing youth. There is a common belief that lengthy, in-depth conversations will allow *all pertinent issues* to be fleshed out, which will in turn lead to better decisions, service plans, and coordination. There is no evidence to support this idea. Beyond a focus on the safety of youth and staff, more does not equal greater benefit to youth. Further, when it comes to what issues are considered pertinent, there is room for debate. A starting point is what kinds of conversations will assist residential staff in helping youth receive the greatest benefit from services.

The point of benefit ought to be front and center of all staffings. We ask, "How will the conversation we are having benefit youth?" An additional way you can evaluate the usefulness of conversations in staffings is to ask yourself, "What can I take away from this conversation that will help me on my next shift (or next interaction with a youth)?" If you cannot identify at least one thing that you will do differently, try harder. Step forward, ask questions. We do not get better by doing more of the things we are already good at. More and more research indicates that with concerted efforts to improve, our growth as professionals stalls very shortly after we begin our careers (Ericsson, Charness, Feltovich, & Hoffman, 2006). We have to work to better ourselves by pushing beyond the edges of our existing ability. Staffings provide a forum for improving our skills because we are not resting on what we already know. We are instead trying to get better by learning something new. Ask, "What do I still need to know about this [youth, situation, etc.] that will help me do my job better?"

As discussed throughout this book, an ongoing challenge for RYCWs is to find a balance when it comes to information. What information do we need to do the job and be effective in our work with youth? What information is interesting but not necessarily helpful? How do we balance intuition with science? Do you trust your gut or rely on standardized processes and questions? There are, of course, no straightforward answers. This is why teams are so vital to the success of residential services. As we have learned, collective decisions are more often better than those made by individuals. But, the caveat is that RYCWs, as part of teams, have to take the onus of speaking up.

What Else *Should RYCWs Do in Staffings?*

Effective teams openly discuss what information to consider in residential staffings. This helps keep conversations focused and, in most cases, more productive. It also communicates respect for everyone's time. In *Thriving on the Front Lines* (Bertolino, 2014), I provided detail about how staffings can be structured in YFS. Here we focus on the role of RYCWs.

First, RYCWs want to be clear on the purpose of services and their role. In addition to the primary focus of safety and other basic needs are the individualized goals for youth as well as outcomes. In Chapter 3 the point of focusing on the outcome of services was discussed. Whereas *goals* reflect specific, concrete behaviors or actions, *outcomes* capture the benefit of services, as evidenced by individual, interpersonal, and social role functioning, from those receiving services. As outlined in the definition of a strengths-based perspective, outcome is measured through routine and ongoing real-time feedback. Real-time feedback requires

80   *We're in This Together*

monitoring both *outcome* and *alliance* (youth and/or supportive others' perceptions of the relationship(s) between themselves and service providers). In staffings, outcome measurement serves a guide for determining the severity of the youth's distress at the start of services, which is the most consistent and reliable predictor of eventual outcome. This point is underscored by research that indicates that mental health professionals are poor at identifying both client progress and deterioration (Bertolino, Bargmann, & Miller, 2013). Outcome can be monitored in staffings with adjustments to services being made based on changes in scores.

RYCWs want to pay attention to whether youth are reporting progress, no progress, or deterioration. Knowing a youth's level of distress helps determine the type and intensity of services and, most importantly, whether services are benefiting youth. We ask not whether youth need services, but rather, are youth benefiting from our services? Monitoring outcome provides a scientific basis for service decisions.

In addition to outcome scores are RYCWs' perceptions of how youth are doing, which are based on their experience, education, and intuition. Because RYCWs are responsible for the day-to-day safety of youth, they will need to use their observational and interviewing skills to identify concerns that may indicate risk (i.e., suicidal ideation, substance abuse, etc.). Staff reports will vary given that staff are trained differently and see things differently. The aim is to identify areas that may indicate risk of harm to self or others and act as hurdles to youth achieving their preferred future. Including staff ratings as part of staffings provides further points of reference and a more encompassing perspective of the youth.

A further area for RYCWs to consider in team meetings and staffings is *action*. Action involves determining *what concerns look like, what to do* to address those concerns or problems, building on positive change and exceptions, and supporting youth and others to achieve positive outcomes. These discussions should include the use of "action-talk." For example, if a youth has a very low score on an outcome measure in which lower scores indicate greater distress, we want to know what is happening in the youth's life that led him or her to provide that rating. In other words, what did a youth say when asked what a certain score represented or "looked like"? Through action-talk we inquire as to what would indicate improvement. Ambiguous language can cause problems in staffings because it can contribute to confusion in terms of what RYCWs and other team members are going to both individually and collectively do to help youth. In worst cases there are threats to safety and well-being, particularly when staff are unclear about their roles and the actions they are expected to carry out.

Clarity and Exception Seeking

Ambiguity in problem descriptions contributes to confusion in terms of what team members are going to both individually and collectively do to help youth. When unclear, it is up to RYCWs to step forward and engage in conversations for clarity. Here is an example of how to do this:

RYCW 1: I think Hillary needs to work on her social skills. She gets scapegoated a lot by the other residents because she says weird things.

RYCW 2: I was thinking the same thing. She really sets herself up with the other youth.

RYCW 3: Okay, you both feel that Hillary needs to work on her social skills. Can you be more specific?

RYCW 1: It's just the weird things she says.

RYCW 3: Since some of us haven't been on shifts where we have witnessed what you have, can you give an example of something weird she has said?

RYCW 2: I can. Well, it wasn't what she said. It was what she did. The other day two other girls were talking, and Hillary started making weird noises. She was squealing, making animal-like sounds.

RYCW 1: Yeah, she did something like that on my shift too. Some of the kids were watching TV, and she went into the room and starting doing this strange dance. She was trying to get their attention, but it just annoyed them. They told her to knock it off, and one of them got so mad he walked out the room. Then Hilary left the room saying, "Everyone hates me!"

RYCW 3: Those are good examples. So it sounds like the way Hillary is trying to make friends, or at least trying to connect with others, is by doing things that instead of attracting others pushes them away. And when she pushes them away, they become annoyed with her and she becomes upset. Is that right?

RYCW 1: I think so. She's going about making friends all wrong.

RYCW 3: Okay. So what we want to do is help Hillary interact better with other youth—whether it's talking or playing games or whatever . . .

RYCW 1: Yes. That's what we want to do.

Whereas working on social skills is a very broad, nondescriptive goal, the idea of "interacting better" moves us closer to a specific goal that every team member understands. Emphasis can then be on ways of helping the youth engage other youth through talking, using posture, eye contact, and so on. We are not searching for right or correct ways of viewing situations; rather, we seek clarity. To gain clarity we make sure to acknowledge the different viewpoints presented as well as any frustration or concerns staff have when they share such feelings.

Occasionally, all parties will not agree as to what constitutes "better" in terms of goals. For instance, a unit manager may want a youth to improve in numerous areas in short order. Meanwhile, a RYCW may feel services will only be successful when the same youth improves her

82 We're in This Together

behavior during the morning routine and at bedtime. Patience and clarity about specific behaviors that are problematic and what "better" will look like in terms of action-talk will typically lead to agreement on goals.

If dissention persists it can be helpful to revisit the purpose of residential services. Our aim is not personality transformation or psychological reprogramming. We are not trying to change the "entire" being of a youth. Instead, first and foremost we create safe environments to meet the baseline needs of youth. Next, we identify the most troublesome concerns—the ones that will likely keep them from the future they want for themselves. By working on specific concerns and improved outcomes, we help youth grow, develop, and have greater well-being (see principle 4, Chapter 1).

Akin to clarity are exceptions. RYCWs will have opportunities in staffings to identify and amply exceptions. By pursuing exceptions, RYCWs are modeling for other staff the importance of emphasizing and building on what is working and times when things are going differently. Times when things are going better indicate the ability of youth to get the upper hand with problems, which indicates resilience, coping ability, and so on. In addition, exceptions are building blocks to larger, future change. Let's continue with the previous example and see how exceptions can be cultivated during a staffing:

RYCW 3: Can someone given an example of a time when Hillary seemed to interact differently—in a better way—with other youth here?

RYCW 2: I was just thinking that she gets along well with Amanda and Courtney. They don't seem to be bothered by her noises and dances. They actually think Hillary's funny sometimes.

LEAD RYCW: [Entering the conversation for the first time] I've seen Hillary use humor too.

RYCW 3: How so? Because sometimes it seems she tries to be funny with noises and dances and it doesn't work, but sometimes it does.

LEAD RYCW: She tells funny stories about her family and people she knows. Maybe that's how she tries to connect with others. I'm not sure.

RYCW 1: I didn't think about it until now, but it makes sense. Sometimes her stories, or, rather, how she acts them out, don't come across the way she wants. But she has made friends here.

RYCW 3: That makes sense. So sometimes her attempts to connect with others work and sometimes they don't. We'd like Hillary to become more successful at making friends and at interacting with others in general. Does that sound right?

[The RYCWs confirm that this is what the group is collectively trying to help Hillary do.]

We're in This Together   83

RYCW 3: For starters, then, we can talk with Hillary about times when she has made friends and what is different about those times when things don't go the way she'd hoped. So we can build on what she is doing that already works and also see if we can expand her repertoire of options for the times it doesn't.

RYCW 2: I agree. And also talk with her about disappointment, because not everyone will want to be friends. And it won't necessarily be because of something's she's done.

[Team members nod their heads in agreement.]

Part of the day-to-day ritual of residential programming involves staff searching for opportunities to respond to even the smallest signs that youth are succeeding or, at least, taking steps forward. This bring us back to our personal philosophies. What do we believe about youth and the prospects of change? We have to *assume* that there will be many example of success—that there will be exceptions to problems. Residential staffings are an excellent context to help RYCWs and other staff orient toward possibilities and positive change, as opposed to the traditional tack of discovering or uncovering deficit and pathology. We engage in strengths-based rather than pathology-based conversations, as detailed in Chapter 2.

There are two further considerations here. First, what might be a few possible benefits of positive change for the youth and the program? This consideration is especially important because many times both RYCWs and youth will be motivated by the benefits—the future visions—that result from making changes. Second, how will we know that youth are benefiting from changes made? What will RYCWs and other staff see happening? A key issue with positive change is identifying and amplifying it. Let's explore these two considerations in the example with Hillary.

RYCW 3: Let's see if we can flesh this out a bit more. What might be a few benefits to Hillary interacting just a little better with the other residents here?

RYCW 1: I think she'll have more friends here . . . and things will be calmer. When she has been upset because it didn't go well with another kid it can take a while for her to calm down.

RYCW 3: Okay. She'll have more friends, and it sounds like things might be calmer for both Hillary and in the program as whole. Let's talk about the benefits to Hillary first. How will we know she is feeling better—what will she be doing?

LEAD RYCW: Smiling more.

RYCW 1: And making eye contact.

RYCW 3: What else?

RYCW 2: I think Hillary will be talking more about her future—like about school, for instance. She really doesn't like school.

84 *We're in This Together*

RYCW 3: It will be great to see all those things more with Hillary. How might her interacting better with other youth here help the program?

RYCW 1: Well, like I said, things will be calmer. And if things are calmer on our shifts, we can spend more time on fun things with the residents and not so much on trying to help her calm down.

RYCW 2: Absolutely. That will be really great!

These kinds of conversations do not have to be extensive to be fruitful. We are also not trying to identify every exception, change every behavior, and get into a guessing game about the future. We are focusing our efforts on those that benefit the individual youth, the other youth on a unit or in a program, and the program at large. In doing so, RYCWs will also benefit.

Sharing News

We want to make every effort to share the results of staffings with youth. One possibility for encouraging youth participation with staffings is to write down various ideas that were generated and sharing them with youth. The following is an example of how this idea might be employed with a youth:

RYCW: Jesse, as you know, we had a staff meeting this morning. Do you remember the form you filled out the other day?

JESSE: The one about things I want staff to know about me?

RYCW: Right. That's the one. Staff were impressed with what you wrote, and we had a chance to talk about it. We also talked about how we might help you accomplish the things you wrote about. Staff had some ideas that I wanted to share with you. Are you interested in hearing them?

JESSE: Yeah.

We want to include youth in decisions—not make promises we are not in a position to follow through on. Interestingly, when we share the outcomes of staffings, youth more often than not will express curiosity. Sometimes they laugh at ideas generated during meetings. Sometimes they ask more questions. And there are times when they say nothing. What matters is the invitation we extend to youth to be as involved as possible.

Further Thoughts on Staffings

Every team must find its collective voice in staffings, when conversations are focused, productive, and inspiring. When conversations drift and are negative, not only are staffings unproductive, but they are

We're in This Together 85

emotionally draining and deflating. In addition to the ideas presented in this chapter about teams, there are other considerations including *time limits* and *simplicity*. By time limits we mean establishing a set amount of time to discuss youth. A common range would be 5–10 minutes, using the three conversational points as a guide. Although there will be exceptions, such as with safety planning, as a rule, longer discussions about youth do not typically translate to better ideas and better outcomes. Time limits also help keep staffings moving, keep discussions focused, ensure that all youth are discussed, and keep staff engaged (Bertolino, 2014).

We also try to keep things simple. Staffings can quickly turn into philosophical or theoretical discussions that may be interesting but more often will complicate matters and be unproductive. Youth are far more interesting to talk about than theories. To be sure that what has been discussed is clear, we ask each staff person to describe, in one minute or less, what he or she will do differently in working with a youth as a result of the conversation. If staff cannot do this, the team as a whole should regroup and revisit its collective decisions.

Wraparound

A final thought about teams relates to *wraparound*, which is not a specific approach but instead a variation on teams. Wraparound involves bringing together trained community personnel for coordinating youth, supportive others, and professionals in the community as a means of empowerment (Sparks & Muro, 2009). Our aim with wraparound teams is to gather persons who can serve as support for youth. Better support systems will provide youth with access to persons who not only care, but who also have experience and knowledge about the world. This can be particularly helpful for youth in less transitional or independent living programs or youth who may be transitioning out of residential programming altogether.

The wraparound process begins with identifying persons who have in the past and/or could in the future contribute to the support of a youth. Potential team members are persons who are relevant to the well-being of the youth (e.g., family members, other natural supports, service providers, and agency representatives). Once possible supports are identified, those persons, if not already involved, are contacted (following appropriate consent). Potential team members are then brought together to discuss the purpose of the wraparound. This includes determining the role that each person might play to support the youth. The team then collaboratively develops an individualized plan of care, implements this plan, and evaluates success over time. The wraparound plan typically includes formal services and interventions, together with community services and interpersonal support and assistance provided by friends, family, and

86 *We're in This Together*

other people drawn from the youth and/or family's social networks. The team convenes frequently to measure the plan's components against relevant indicators of success. Plan components and strategies are revised when outcomes are not being achieved.

The overall wraparound process of engaging the youth and/or family, convening the team, developing the plan, implementing the plan, and transitioning the youth out of formal wraparound is typically facilitated by a RYCW or other YFS staff who is considered the "wraparound facilitator." The facilitator is sometimes assisted by a family support worker. The wraparound process, and the plan itself, is designed to be culturally competent, strengths based, and organized around family members' own perceptions of needs, goals, and the likelihood of success of specific strategies (Bertolino, 2014).

Hands to Hands: Shift Changes

Residential programs tend vary in how they coordinate staff transitions. Some require incoming staff to review progress notes on the youth in the program. In others there are brief updates between incoming and outgoing staff. And some programs try to ensure that there is at least one "up-to-date" staff person who remains (i.e., has been on shift for a few hours) as new ones start their shifts. This way someone is always in the know.

Youth do not fall through the cracks in YFS. Rather, they slip through people's fingers. Shift changes represent both opportunities and pitfalls. If approached and coordinated well, shift changes are opportunities for RYCWs to build cohesion and vision. Specific opportunities during shift changes include discussion of these elements:

- Problem areas or situations, including what has been tried but has not worked, what has worked (including partial successes), and what might work but has not been tried;
- General tasks or activities used by RYCWs or staff that helped make a positive difference for the youth; and,
- Exceptions that were observed by RYCWs or other staff and how those exceptions can be further developed and amplified on the upcoming shift.

There are also exploratory questions that can help incoming RYCWs to determine what went right on a previous shift or day:

- What did you notice happening during your shift that you'd like to have continue?
- What things did you notice each resident do that might be an indication that that he or she in making progress toward a goal?

We're in This Together   87

- What were the highlights of your shift?
- What specifically did you do to help things to remain manageable, calm, and pleasant?
- What was inspiring about your shift?
- What words of wisdom do you have to guide me through this shift?

Questions such as these help RYCWs "take the temperature" of the program at large while also collecting bits of information about individual youth. Being proactive through questioning can assist with creating a climate of success as opposed to one in which RYCWs feel they are always "putting out fires." As an adjunct, Table 4.5, "Staff Shift Change Form," provides a written way of communicating crucial information in the event that there is limited time to have a verbal exchange. This form can be completed by one or more staff in less than 5 minutes prior to the end of a shift.

Shift changes need not be extensive. A brief, focused conversation can beneficial. The key is for RYCWs to practice shift change exchanges so that there is a working structure in place.

"I'm Fried": Countering Frustration During Shift Changes

There is good reason that residential programs struggle mightily to keep frontline staff such as RYCWs. For reasons described in Chapter 1, RYCWs are the "go-to" staff—much rests on their shoulders. And it's not uncommon for unchecked frustrations to surface during shift changes. For example, if a RYCW says, "Everything was fine. See ya!" or "They're all yours, good luck!" or "I gotta go. I'm fried" and then runs for the door, that is an indication that frustration is knocking. More commonly there are staff who stay around long enough to run through a shift change, but they are so worn out or worn down that staff exchanges are unhelpful.

Let's consider a few ways to better manage shift changes when frustration is looming. For incoming RYCWs, keep in mind that when outgoing staff are emotionally drained, there is a greater likelihood that shift changes will have a negative tone. Do not be hypnotized into the belief that "bad means bad" and "good means good." Ask specific questions to get specific information that will help you on your shift. Ask yourself, "What do I need to know to do my job as best as possible?" In addition, acknowledge and validate as you listen. This will help soften the experience. You will appreciate being on the recipient end when the tables are turned and you are leaving as another RYCW is coming in. What follows is an example of how an incoming RYCW might acknowledge, validate, and gather information in a conversation with an outgoing RYCW:

OUTGOING (O) RYCW: I'm glad you're here. It's been a rough night. I've been going out of my mind. I need to get out of here. I'm so frustrated.

Table 4.5 Staff Shift Change Form

Staff Shift Change Form

Staff Member(s) on Duty:

Staff Member Completing This Form:

Date:

Time of Shift:

1. On a scale of 1 to 10, with 1 being as poor as things could be and 10 being as good as things could be in the program at this time, how would you rate things?

   _____

   What is currently happening to warrant your rating?

   _____

2. What would need to happen for things to improve just a little (e.g., a half point) from the rating you gave? _____

3. What specific things did you or other staff do that didn't work too well, worked to some degree, or might work but you didn't try? _____

   _____

   _____

4. What did you notice happening during your shift that you would like to have continue to happen on this and upcoming shifts? _____

   _____

   _____

5. What kinds of things did you or other staff do during the shift to keep things manageable, calm, and pleasant? _____

   _____

   _____

6. Is there anything else that might be helpful for ongoing staff to know?

   _____

   _____

We're in This Together   89

INCOMING (I) RYCW: I'm sorry it's been a rough night. You sound exhausted. What happened?

O-RYCW: I am exhausted. Totally. All the kids were acting up. It was nuts.

I-RYCW: Okay. I don't want to delay you leaving, so can I ask just a few quick questions so I have a better idea of what's been going on and what I can do?

O-RYCW: Sure.

I-RYCW: Thanks. I'll be brief. So it seemed that all the kids were acting up. Can you say more about what you mean by that?

O-RYCW: Well, I guess it wasn't all the kids. It just seemed like that because it was so chaotic.

I-RYCW: I've had shifts like that too. So who was doing what?

O-RYCW: It was Hector, James, and Lonnie. Hector and James had a loud shouting match, and Lonnie was egging them on by calling them names.

I-RYCW: I can see why you said it was "chaotic." What did you do?

O-RYCW: I was able to get Lonnie's attention and have him leave the room. Then Hector and James said a couple more things to each other, then James walked away from it and Hector stopped too.

I-RYCW: That was a good idea to get Lonnie's attention and get him out of the room. It could have been much worse. What happened after that?

O-RYCW: I talked with Hector and James, and they apologized to each other. Things were calm after that. All this happened just about an hour ago.

I-RYCW: So your shift was generally calm until an hour ago?

O-RYCW: Totally.

I-RYCW: Wow. How did you and Stephanie [the other outgoing RYCW] keep things going so well before the incident?

O-RYCW: We played games this afternoon and did a community group meeting. It was fun.

I-RYCW: I don't know all these kids, just a few. Any thoughts about what I can do to set the kind of tone you and Stephanie did earlier on your shift?

O-RYCW: Just spend time getting to know them. They are an open group but probably won't just tell you how they're feeling unless you ask.

I-RYCW: Anything I should avoid doing?

O-RYCW: Yes, I would not recommend sitting back and seeing how things unfold. This group, as a whole, likes to be engaged. They like to do things. So I would do some activities with them, and then give them time to wind down before lights out. A half hour should be enough time for them to settle down.

I-RYCW: Thanks for the help. Have a great night.

Much of the frustration that RYCWs experience can be neutralized though genuineness and regard for what peers have experienced. We

90   We're in This Together

listen carefully, acknowledging and validating while moving conversations forward as quickly as possible through focused questions. We ask about what worked and what did not and make sure that whatever was learned is shared with other staff who may also be beginning their shifts. Then we pass along what we learned during our shifts to those who will take over as our shifts come to an end.

Checking in With Youth

Following a shift change and tasks that need immediate attention, it is a good idea to check in with youth. Doing so is an opportunity to greet everyone, meet any new residents, and take the collective pulse of the group. It's also a chance to take note of any youth who seem to be struggling or seem to be in an especially good mood. A specific way of engaging youth is to say, "Who can tell me one good thing that has happened today?" Asking questions such as this can establish a tone for the shift, and if things have not been going particularly well, it can change the mood of the residents. Another possibility is to talk individually with youth and search for exceptions and/or examples of positive moments from which to build. Here is an example of how to do this:

RYCW: Hi Samantha! How have you been?

SAMANTHA: Okay, I guess. But Kayla better back off or she's gonna get it.

RYCW: What's bothering you about Kayla?

SAMANTHA: She's getting on my nerves. She keeps saying shit about me behind my back to the other girls. I'm mad.

RYCW: You're concerned that maybe Kayla's said some things about you to the other girls.

SAMANTHA: Yep.

RYCW: I can see why that might make you mad. Thanks for talking with me about it. I'm wondering how you have managed to keep it together and tell me about it rather than acting on your feelings. How have you done that?

SAMANTHA: I just say she's not worth it.

RYCW: To yourself or to Kayla?

SAMANTHA: To myself. I don't say anything back to her because she'll just lie and say she didn't do it when I know she did.

RYCW: Samantha, that is an excellent decision. How does telling yourself "she's not worth it" help you?

SAMANTHA: Because then I remember that it's not worth getting into trouble and maybe getting kicked out.

RYCW: It sounds like you see a very good reason to be here and not let something like that risk your stay. Is that right?

SAMANTHA: Yeah. I want to get into the TLP [Transitional Living Program] and they won't consider me if I get into a fight.

RYCW: I'm glad to hear you are interested in TLP. How can Mark [the other RYCW on shift] and I support you tonight while we are here?

SAMANTHA: I'm not sure.

RYCW: How did staff on the last shift help?

SAMANTHA: Jordan talked to me a couple of times during her shift.

RYCW: Jordan checked in with you every once in a while?

SAMANTHA: Yeah, just a couple times.

RYCW: Would it help if I checked in with you? Or Mark, if that would be better for you.

SAMANTHA: That would help—either you or Mark is fine.

Again, acknowledgment, validation, and exception seeking, fueled by patience, will help RYCWs connect with youth, diffuse potentially unstable situations, and identify strengths to use throughout present and future shifts. We can also guide conversations more deliberately toward "what's working" by asking youth, "Tell me about what's better since the last time I worked" or "I'd like to hear about all the good things you've been up to since we last saw each other." Then, when we hear about exceptions, we follow up with, "How did you that?" and "How can you do that a little more?" and "How can we help you with that?"

In this chapter we explored the role of teams in residential programs. Although this chapter is just the "tip of the iceberg" in terms of the ways teams function in residential care, it provides some guidance for RYCWs. In the next chapter, we will learn about numerous strategies that RYCWs can use to assist youth in moving toward their goals, achieving future visions, and gaining the most benefit for our programs.

5 There's More Than One Way
Strategies for Change

One of the frequent requests made by RYCWs, and frontline staff for that matter, is for more training on strategies—methods, techniques, and interventions for working with youth in residential settings. This is a reasonable request, and yet by now hopefully you are beginning to experience some skepticism that simply learning more methods will improve our effectiveness as RYCWs. You may even be questioning whether more training is the answer. And ironically, research suggests that more training may actually have a negative effect on the performance of mental health professionals. But there is good news. As it turns out, *some* forms of training do make more of a difference in RYCW effectiveness and youth outcomes than others. One type of training that matters is that which is based on research about the alliance-outcomes correlation. That is, better relationships (alliances) yield better outcomes. Recall that the definition of strengths based and the five principles outlined in the first chapter are founded on decades of research on both the alliance and outcomes. What we have learned is that effective strategies are based on this research rather than on research on specific models. Our allegiances are with youth, not our models.

In this chapter we will learn about specific methods for working with youth in residential programs. And as we explore these options, we keep in mind that the choice of methods should not be random. Instead, we use the strengths-based principles described in Chapter 1 as the foundation for choosing methods that both fit and provide the greatest possibility of benefit to youth.

Here we explore two overarching pathways to facilitate change with youth. The first is by helping youth and supportive others to change their views. *Views* include cognitions, thoughts, ideas, perceptions, beliefs, evaluations, interpretations, attention, and identity stories. The second pathway is *actions and interactions*, which refer to patterns of behavior and patterns of interaction. Interventions aimed at changing views can be used with most youth whereas those that target behavior and interactions are typically contingent on how youth see themselves in relation to concerns.

Positive Youth Development (PYD)

Methods should be purposeful. We want to meet the needs of youth, target specific goals, and improve overall functioning. One way to promote well-being is through Positive Youth Development (PYD). PYD is an ongoing process of engaging youth in safe, secure environments through activities, interventions, and programs that promote growth, development, and overall well-being. One way to measure the success of residential care in YFS is by measuring the degree to which youth achieve improved functioning as evidenced by the following nine outcomes of PYD:

1. Rewarding bonding
2. Fostering resilience
3. Promoting social, emotional, cognitive, behavioral, and moral competence
4. Fostering self-determination
5. Fostering spirituality
6. Fostering clear and positive identity
7. Building belief in the future
8. Providing recognition for positive behavior
9. Providing opportunities for prosocial development
10. Fostering prosocial norms (Catalano, Berglund, Ryan, Lonczak, & Hawkins, 2004)

The strategies offered in this chapter help youth develop the skills they need to flourish by reducing negative symptoms *and* by building positive emotions, purpose or meaning, positive relationships, and positive accomplishments, all of which are considered pillars of Positive Psychology, the forerunner to PYD (Seligman, 2011).

Considerations for Using Strategies

Before we delve in the two primary pathways, let's consider, briefly, how to increase the effectiveness of strategies through *fit* and *effect*, two ongoing considerations for RYCWs in determining how attempts to facilitate change are working. The points of discussion that follow are described in detail in the companion book, *Thriving on the Front Lines* (Bertolino, 2014).

Does the Method Fit?

A first area of consideration is *fit*. By *fit* we mean if the chosen intervention is appropriate for the youth. Does it fit the youth's worldview, culture, and ideas about change? To increase the fit of interventions, we consider factors that build on strengths and resources, create rapport, are culturally sensitive, and increase well-being.

94 *There's More Than One Way*

One place to start is by exploring how youth and supportive others align themselves with the problems and concerns that are a focus of services. This is because youth and supportive others will express varying degrees of association with concerns. For example, some youth will say they are responsible for the entirety of problems with statements such as, "I'm the one who stole the car" or "I know things can't go on like this." Some youth will refuse involvement and perhaps assign responsibility to others for concerns/problems, stating, "It's their fault" or "I didn't do anything." Others will align themselves with some portion or aspect of concerns: "We both did it" or "We sometimes make bad decisions."

An additional way to better understand associations youth and supportive others may have with concerns can be found with their use of pronouns such as "I," "me," "mine," "my," "we," "us," "our," "you," "he/she," "him/her," and "they/them." When any of the first seven pronouns listed are used, youth and supportive others are likely indicating some level of involvement with their concerns/problems. The absence of self, by using pronouns such as "you," "he/she," or "they/them," can indicate distancing from problems. Because youth self-references are embedded in context, RYCWs must remain aware that various pronouns mean different things in different cultures (e.g., the use of "you" by some Hispanic youth may include themselves: "When you get up in the morning, you need to have your homework finished."). Finally, the following questions can assist with exploring how youth situate themselves and others in relationship to presenting concerns:

- Who would you say is involved with this concern/problem?
- What would you say is your part, if any, in all of this?
- What's your role, if any, in what's going on?
- On a scale of 1 to 10, how involved would you say you are with the concern/problem?
- In your estimation, who needs to do what about the concern/problem?

Information from these questions can help with choosing interventions. For example, youth and supportive others who see themselves as having little or no role problems are unlikely to do anything different to change their situations. Interventions should therefore be aimed at helping youth change their views or perspectives, which is the focus of this chapter. On the other hand, youth who more closely align themselves with problems are likely to be more amenable to changing their behavior or how they to relate to others. In these cases we can employ interventions that emphasize changing views *and/or* those that encourage action.

These questions also reveal hints about how youth expect things to change in their lives with current situations but also about their coping style. Coping style indicates whether youth tend to be more internalized or externalized both in how they deal with stress and difficulty and solving problems. Knowing whether a particular youth is more or less introverted or extroverted assists with the choice of intervention. For example, youth with internalized coping styles may benefit more from methods that focus on internal experience such as feelings and thoughts whereas youth with externalized coping styles are likely to respond better to methods that focus on behavior or action. In addition to coping style, RYCWs are cognizant that youth will vary in terms of emotional, intellectual, and physical ability. We consider factors that might affect a youth's comprehension and ability to respond to an intervention. To increase the prospects of effectiveness, we consider the developmental fit of interventions, steering clear of "one-size-fits-all" methods (Bertolino, 2014).

A final area related to fit includes asking "orienting" questions, which offer a glimpse of how youth have experienced change in their lives in past situations. The following questions can serve as a guide:

- How do things usually change in your life?
- What prompts or initiates change in your life?
- How do you usually try to resolve your concerns/problems?
- What have you done in the past to resolve your concerns/problems?
- What ideas do you have about how change might happen with your concern/problem/situation?
- If someone you know had this concern/problem/situation, what would you suggest he or she do to resolve it?
- What has to happen before the change you are seeking can occur?
- At what rate (i.e., slow or fast, over days or months, etc.) do you think change will occur?
- Do you expect change to occur by seeing things differently? By doing something different? By others doing something different?
- What thoughts or ideas have you been considering about how this problem has come about and what might put it to rest?
- Given your ideas about the problem, what do you think would be the first step in addressing it?
- What might you do differently as a result of the thoughts or ideas you've developed?
- If you had this thought or idea about someone else, what would you suggest that he or she do to resolve it?

It is usually not necessary to ask more than a few questions to gather information about a particular concern. The point is to do our best to consider those variables that are likely to increase the probability to positive change. To our questions some youth will answer, "I don't know." This kind of response need not be a deterrent. Questions are invitations to share information, not inquisitions into the lives of youth—which they are often used to from adults. If no information is gleaned, say, "Okay.

96 *There's More Than One Way*

I just thought I would ask. Please let me know if anything comes to mind." At that point the RYCW does his or her best to select interventions that best fit the youth and the situation.

What Is the Effect of the Method?

Effect refers to outcome. We ask: Did the intervention, at minimum, benefit the youth (e.g., keep a situation from getting worse, increase self-worth, etc.) or, at best, lead to a positive, measurable outcome? All attempts to promote change should also involve feedback. We want to know: What were the results? What was the youth's experience in the situation in which the intervention was used? And finally, don't be afraid to fail. If something doesn't work, learn from it.

There are two general categories that help determine effect: *no improvement or deterioration* and *improvement*. If a method does not produce benefit, we respond sooner rather than later. If there are indicators of positive change, we continue the intervention.

In evaluating effect, RYCWs attend to two forms of information. The first relates to what youth communicate verbally and nonverbally through language and interaction. For example, does a youth talk about things as if they are better? Unchanged? Worse? What can be drawn from the youth's body language? As described throughout this book, youth will often give vague, nondescriptive answers, which calls for YCWs to use action-talk to gain clarity.

A second level of information RYCWs attend to is the ongoing distress of youth as captured through outcome measurement. We want to learn through instrumentation whether or not things are improving and whether or not services provided are of benefit. As discussed earlier in this book, in initial sessions and meetings, youth are asked to complete an outcome measure. The measure is then scored, and the results and meaning of those scores is discussed. RYCWs also use outcome measurement to monitor distress, particularly through sharp increases or decreases. Although we strive for early change, with few exceptions (i.e., so-called "epiphanies" or life-changing experiences) change that "sticks" tends to be gradual. When large increases or decreases occur, RYCWs will want to consider further risk assessment (Bertolino, 2014). Large changes should be followed up quickly.

No improvement means that a youth has expressed a continuation of roughly the same degree of distress (within a predefined range) and/or well-being based on formal instrumentation, verbal statements by youth, or staff observation. With the latter, youth will usually provide statements such as, "Things are the same as last time" or "There's nothing new." It should be noted that formal instrumentation is considered more reliable but does not replace the observation skills of RYCWs.

Deterioration indicates that a youth has expressed an increased degree of distress (within a predefined range) and/or well-being based on

There's More Than One Way 97

formal instrumentation, verbal statements by youth, or staff observation. Research makes it clear that mental health practitioners often struggle to identify deterioration. This finding underscores the importance of RYCWs using formal outcome measurement, which reduces the chances that deterioration will go unnoticed.

Youth who are deteriorating will typically verbalize their distress with statements such as, "My life is going downhill," "My life sucks," or "It's worse than before." Reports of this kind are not unusual because youth will have ups and downs, so it is important that RYCWs explore the meaning of both outcome scores and youth comments. It is especially important to respond to deterioration as it is highly correlated with frustration and loss of hope, which are precursors for dropout (Garcia & Weisz, 2002) and negative outcome (Warren et al., 2012), two of the most significant threats to YFS as a whole.

Improvement indicates that a youth has expressed a decrease in the degree of distress (within a predefined range) and/or improvement in well-being based on formal instrumentation, verbal statements by youth, or staff observation. Monitoring progress from the outset of services means we are not only able to distinguish youth who are reporting no improvement or deterioration but those who are rating their lives and situations as improved. RYCWs want to explore any form of positive change as it may serve as a building block to more significant, sweeping changes. In contrast, change that is considered reliable and valid will have to be measured formally, which is another reason for a residential program to commit to standardized outcome measurement.

How RYCWs and other residential staff involved respond to situations involving no improvement and deterioration can be the difference between a youth staying engaged long enough to reap the benefit of services and dropping out. If youth drop out, we may not have another chance to help them, and, perhaps worse, they may shy away from future mental health services, believing that it won't do any good. When faced with deterioration, YCWs must be prepared to respond in a swift and deliberate manner (Bertolino, 2014). Similarly, responses to improvement are all crucial in determining next steps in residential services. We will return to these two categories of responses in Chapter 7.

In just a moment, we will delve into key interventions for changing views, actions, and interactions. A final thought is for RYCWs to avoid becoming formulaic in their choices of methods. One-size-fits-all methods inevitably fail. This is because decisions about interventions are made void of the most influential contributors to outcome—youth. By focusing on fit and effect, RYCWs will have the creativity necessary to make choices of strategies that improve the likelihood of success.

Whether it's developing rapport, attending to expectations, or changing language, we are trying to facilitate change and in doing so positively affect the present and the future. With this in mind, the methods

98　*There's More Than One Way*

that follow are used to facilitate growth, development, well-being, or some hoped-for goal or outcome. We work *toward* some form of change rather than trying to move away from or escape something (e.g., shifting attention to what has worked rather than what has not). In other words, we seek the presence rather than the absence of things. We also keep in mind that to increase the probability that the methods described in this chapter will work, they have to fit with youth and the context or situation. There are many choices in terms of methods and techniques, but the research is clear that the most effective RYCWs follow the principles in Chapter 2 as the foundation for any intervention. So while there may be an inclination to skip straight to methods—"what to do"—doing so undermines the very factors most responsible for change and growth (Bertolino, 2014).

Pathway 1: Changing Views

Just how do youth and their supportive others contribute to sustain problems? The following story helps us better understand this:

A major league baseball player was having a "breakout" season. He was leading the league in batting average and had far surpassed both his and the team's preseason expectation of his performance. Just after the midseason all-star break, the player began to struggle. At first it seemed that he just had a string of unproductive at bats. But soon his struggles turned into a full-fledged slump. The player could not believe that things had changed so quickly. He was at a loss to figure out what went wrong.

Given the video technology, he had available every at bat he had taken, so the player got to work dissecting his recent plate appearances. As he watched himself striking out and hitting weak ground balls, he immediately identified the problem. He noticed that he had been pulling off pitches. Instead of keeping his head steady and his eyes firmly on the ball as it entered the strike zone, he was pulling his head up and away from the ball. He also became aware that he was moving his feet too much in the batter's box. Aware of the errors with his approach to hitting, the player got to work to make the necessary corrections.

To the player's surprise, despite the corrections, he continued to struggle at the plate. The strikeouts were now piling up, and he was becoming more and more despondent about his play. So he returned to watching video only to find that he had missed a few things. He now noticed that he was lunging at pitches rather than keeping his weight back. He simultaneously became aware that he was standing too close to the plate. He *now* knew what to correct.

He had a new plan—it just didn't work. His struggles continued. Back to the video room he went. He vowed to find the problems with his batting. He had to be missing something.

One evening, as he was watching video, a coach stopped by. The coach said, "I know you have been watching video, trying to identify what's wrong with your approach to hitting. I admire your passion and perseverance. And now I'd like you to reconsider your overall approach."

The player replied, "Coach, that's what I've been trying to do—to reconsider my overall approach—because what I have been doing with my hitting hasn't worked. I've found a lot of things I can do better, but I still haven't found the one thing that will fix everything."

"That's not what I mean," countered the coach. "You have spent hours and hours watching yourself underperform—swinging and missing, popping up pitches you would typically hammer. You are becoming an expert on poor performance. What I suggest is you start watching video of yourself making the kind of swings you are capable of. Watch video of earlier this season, before the all-star break, when you were hitting line drives and pitchers couldn't get you out. Identify what you were doing right, the things that were working with your approach to hitting. Then go out and do those things instead of trying to fix this or that." The player followed the coach's advice, and within a few games he was back on track with his hitting.

The baseball player was not holding a wrong view, just an unhelpful one. His view was to identify problems with his hitting and then take corrective actions to get his swing back on track. Sometimes this kind of approach works. We identify a problem and fix it. But frequently this perspective does not work. In fact, it may even make things worse. What is needed is a different perspective, one that builds on already existing strengths and resources and presents more options. The coach did just this.

But let's consider the two very different philosophies used. First, the player assumed that identification of what he was doing wrong as a hitter would provide him with answers for fixing his swing. So the theory is, find the problem, correct the problem, and have an improved outcome. The coach's approach was to find examples of success—either in the present or the past. Study those successes, identify what you are capable of and times when you have been successful. Then import what has been learned into your present performance.

The two perspectives described through example are not the only possibilities for viewing a situation. And yet, what becomes clear is that a focus on strengths and what's working provides far more opportunities for success than when the focus is on pathology and what's wrong.

O'Hanlon and Weiner-Davis (2003) suggest that a change in views can lead to changes in action as well as the stimulation of unused potentials and resources. This idea can be especially useful for RYCWs, as the generation of a new view can lead to a small shift in an attentional pattern, thereby leading to new and creative ideas for working with youth.

Problematic Stories

One of the ways to identify problematic views is through stories. There are times when youth and supportive others will develop stories about youth that reflect negativity, pessimism, blame, apathy, and loss of hope

100 *There's More Than One Way*

and, as a result, will close down possibilities for positive change. These kinds of stories are referred to as *problem saturated* (White & Epston, 1990). We keep in mind that any kind of story can change, with problem-saturated ones being a target of residential services.

How do we identify problematic stories? Listen for descriptions of youth that imply, suggest, or directly impart *impossibility* ("He'll never change"), *blame* ("It's all her fault"), *invalidation* ("You shouldn't feel that way"), or *nonaccountability* ("I can't help myself"). Consider the following example:

> Steven was a teenager who lived in Phoenix and had become a member of the Flaming Arrow Patrol of Ingleside's Troop 294 in the late 1950s and early 1960s. One of the parents who supervised Steven and the group of boys in the troop was a man named Dick Hoffman. Over time Hoffman developed an image of young Steven:

> He seemed to go in fits and starts—he would dash from one thing to another. I thought it was a disability, not being able to concentrate the way the rest of us would. I knew he was wildly enthusiastic, but I didn't think he had enough ability to analyze things . . . I thought, "When he grows up and gets into the real world he's going to have a tough time keeping up." I didn't dream anything would come of him.
> (McBride, 1997, pp. 77–78).

Does this kind of youth sound familiar? Perhaps today this young man would be labeled as "easily distractible," "has difficulty staying focused," or "cannot complete tasks in a timely manner." He might even be diagnosed with ADHD and be put on medication. The young man? Director and producer Steven Spielberg. Sometime later Hoffman would say about his perception of Steven as a teenager, "Of course, that was a complete misjudgment of the kid's personality" (p. 78).

A common characteristic of problem-saturated stories is that they create a mirage or smoke screen for RYCWs. Problematic stories are deceiving in that they appear as "real" depictions—so real that RYCWs become entranced by them. We want to recognize that what actually exists behind these mirages are youth who are more than any one story or narrative. There are many, many stories that wind together and make up the lives of youth. Instead of becoming participants in the problematic stories that often surround youth, as RYCWs, we challenge or cast doubt upon them and develop new stories of hope and possibilities. To do this we focus on changing views. Let's now explore some ways of doing this.

Changing Views Through Exception Seeking

The main method of changing views available to RYCWs involves searching for exceptions. Recall from earlier chapters that exceptions represent moments when problems are less influential, more manageable, or absent

There's More Than One Way   101

altogether. Exceptions also include times when problems were expected to occur or get worse and did not. By identifying moments when youth and supportive others have more influence over problems, we highlight ability and coping skills and promote resilience. There are multiple ways of both identifying and building on exceptions.

RYCWs exercise caution with exception-oriented questions, seeking small differences between times when problems get the upper hand with youth and when youth get the better of problems. Root questions to explore for exceptions are as follows:

- When is the problem not a problem?
- Think about a time when the problem did not happen. What was different about that time?
- What do you notice about the times when [the problem] is less of a problem? What is different?
- What is different about the times that [the problem] is less noticeable?
- How far back would you have to go to find a time that [the problem] was less dominant in your life? What do you recall about that time?
- Tell me about a time that you expected [the problem] to happen but it didn't. What happened instead?
- What is different about the times when things go a little better?

"All-or-nothing" questions (i.e., the problem happened or did not happen) are avoided as some youth or supportive others will have difficulty identifying times when problems were absent. They will respond, "The problem always happens. There aren't any times when it's better." A further consequence is that some clients will experience invalidation, feeling that the RYCW is glossing over the severity of the problem or situation. In such cases we further acknowledge and simultaneously search for smaller exceptions. The following is an example of how to do this:

YOUTH: I never do anything right.

RYCW: Your sense is you haven't done anything right. Can you give me an example of what you mean?

YOUTH: I keep getting in trouble because I haven't been doing my homework.

RYCW: So you've had some trouble because sometimes you haven't done your homework. When was the most recent time that you got some part of your homework done?

YOUTH: Well, not last night, but the night before I got English and geometry done but not world history.

RYCW: How were you able to get that much of your homework done?

YOUTH: I started on it earlier. But I still didn't have enough time.

RYCW: Okay, I want to come back to that because it's important. But one other question first. Before two nights ago, when was the last time you got at least part of your homework completed?

102 There's More Than One Way

YOUTH: The night before that. Most nights I get some homework done but not all of it.

RYCW: That's excellent. You've done well to get a good portion done even if it hasn't been all of it. When was the last time you got all your homework done?

YOUTH: Last Tuesday [one week ago].

RYCW: Awesome! What was different about last Tuesday?

YOUTH: I had enough time.

RYCW: Okay, so going back to what you said earlier and also looking at last Tuesday, if you have enough time, more times than not you get your homework done.

YOUTH: Yeah.

The point of exceptions is to find moments when youth are using their abilities in the service of problem resolution. And yet, oftentimes strengths are masked by problem-saturated stories. In the previous example, the RYCW searched for exceptions by starting in the present and working backward to find times when things had gone differently regarding homework. The rational for starting in the present is that in most cases the more current the exception, the stronger its influence.

The RYCW also sought examples of getting "some" rather than all homework completed. Once evidence was found, time was spent developing the exception further. Particularly important is not *why* the youth got homework done at times, but *how* he did it. In this case time was a factor. A goal of the RYCW then would be to help the youth secure the time necessary to complete homework.

An additional note relates to the use of language as a vehicle for change, as described in Chapter 3. This was done by combining acknowledgment with possibility. The RYCW introduced possibility through perceptual changes ("your sense is"), past tense ("haven't done anything," "had some trouble"), and partiality ("sometimes you haven't done your homework").

A further consideration regarding exceptions is that it is generally easier to evoke past abilities such as exceptions than to teach youth something they have never done. For example, if a youth is trying to resolve a conflict, we want to search for times in the past when he or she had been successful in that area (to any degree) and then build on the ability by linking it to the present problem situation or context. If an exception is within the youth's experience, it becomes an ability as opposed to a deficit or something that has to be taught. This can be especially helpful when trying to teach conflict resolution, anger management, or assertiveness training, for example.

Building Accountability Through Exceptions

A second way to build exceptions is by using acknowledgment in combination with accountability. We focus on accountability due to its importance

There's More Than One Way   103

in virtually every aspect of life. We want our public figures, corporations, and communities to take responsibility for their actions. Likewise, each of us must accept responsibility for ourselves, and we endeavor to communicate this to youth.

In Chapter 3 we learned of ways to use language to acknowledge, validate, and introduce the element of possibility into otherwise closed-down situations. These methods provide respectful, subtle inroads for promoting new views. Larger changes often emerge through smaller ones that are initiated through language. Here we focus on a series of methods to use acknowledgment to promote personal agency (in other words, responsibility and accountability).

Youth (and sometimes others involved with services) at times attempt to rationalize actions or behaviors by attributing them to genetics, physiology, development, relationships (interpersonal), family, personality, or other influences. Although such influences can shape behavior, with few exceptions (i.e., certain intellectual and developmental disabilities) they do not cause it. Statements of accountability are reflections of views. We therefore use language as a means of both inviting accountability by acknowledging the experiences of youth and identifying exceptions— times when accountability has been present but perhaps gone unnoticed. Next are several ways to do this.

Reflect Back Nonaccountability Statements Without the Nonaccountability Part

Example 1   YOUTH: If he hadn't called me a name, I wouldn't have hit him.
RYCW: You hit him.
Example 2   YOUTH: She pissed me off, so I took off.
YCW: You got mad and ran away.
Example 3   YOUTH: I didn't get my medication on time, so I didn't remember to do my homework.
YCW: You didn't do your homework.

Use the Word "and" to Link Internal Experience and Accountability

Reflect back what youth are experiencing internally and link it to what they are accountable for. To do this, RYCWs use the word "and" instead of "but." This does two things. It lets youth know that the RYCW is not trying to change how they feel. Next, it holds youth accountable for what they do—their actions and behaviors.

Example 1   YOUTH: He makes me so mad. That's why I hit him.
RYCW: You can be mad, and it's not okay to hit him or anyone else.

104 *There's More Than One Way*

Example 2 YOUTH: I can't help it. I just can't stop scratching my arm.

RYCW: You can feel as if you can't help it, and there are options other than scratching your arm.

Example 3 YOUTH: My family is all depressed alcoholics. So when I am down, I get wasted.

RYCW: It's okay to get down and sometimes you may feel depressed, and it's not okay to drink to try and cope with things that way.

Identify Counterexamples That Indicate Choice or Accountability

A third way to promote a change in viewing through language and invite accountability is to search for exceptions to the actions or behavior for which youth are not claiming accountability. Aside from certain identified conditions, RYCWs can make generalizations here because it is impossible for youth to behave negatively 24 hours a day. Once exceptions have been identified, they can be amplified.

Example 1 YOUTH: I can't help it. I was abused when I was little, so that's how I learned to deal with my anger.

RYCW: I'm curious. You got angry with your unit supervisor yesterday, and you didn't scream at her. How did you handle your anger differently?

Example 2 YOUTH: When I get angry, I can't think clearly and take off. That's what happens when you have ADHD.

RYCW: Sometimes it seems harder than others for you to focus, and I'm curious, how come you don't take off every time you get angry?

Example 3 YOUTH: The teacher is just going to flunk me anyway, so why should I do any homework?

RYCW: I must be missing something. How did you manage to get some passing grades earlier this semester?

Accountability is important to life but especially so in residential settings given the prevalence of psychiatric diagnoses. As we have learned, labels have both pros and cons and have changed with time, influenced by economics and culture (Whitaker, 2010). In addition, youth often receive messages, sometimes from the very mental health professionals who are supposed to help, that they are incapable of things (e.g., regulating their emotions, learning new things, having the futures they want, etc.). We counter these ideas in two ways. The first is through person-first language, which, as we learned in the first chapter, serves as a reminder to always see youth as human beings, not as labels. Second, we search for exceptions. With both elements we communicate to youth that not only are they people but that what we are trying to change are actions and behaviors, not diagnoses and labels.

There's More Than One Way 105

A final consideration with accountability relates to the use psycho-tropic medication. Because medications are commonly prescribed to youth in residential programs, it is imperative that RYCWs receive training. By understanding the purpose of psychotropic medication, including what they are *supposed* to do and potential side effects, RYCWs can promote accountability with youth.

As noted in the aforementioned examples, an often unforeseen "side effect" of medication (and psychiatric labels) is the sense that the medication is responsible for behavior as well as any subsequent changes, positive or negative. Our job as RYCWs is to invite accountability. Let's consider a further options for inviting accountability through exception seeking when a youth is taking psychotropic medication. This method involves finding out from youth what percentage of their behavior is due to them being "in charge" as opposed to their medication (Bertolino, 1999).

(Words in *italics* are verbally emphasized by the RYCW.)

YOUTH: My medication calms me down so I can control myself.
RYCW: It makes you *feel* calmer, right?
YOUTH: Yeah.
RYCW: So when you feel like you're more in control, what are you doing?
YOUTH: I don't hit things or break things.
RYCW: How do you get yourself to do that?
YOUTH: I just stop myself.
RYCW: That has me curious. I haven't come across a medication that makes decisions for people or actually takes control of what they do. For you, what percentage of being in control do you think is because of things you're doing, and what percentage is due to the medication?
YOUTH: I guess it's 60% me and 40% my Adderall and Klonopin.
RYCW: What does that 60% of you do to help you make better decisions and stay in control?
YOUTH: I just keep telling myself that I can do it. I can stay in control.
RYCW: So the medication helps you *feel calmer* but *it is you* who is in charge and makes decisions and *chooses* to stay in control?
YOUTH: Yeah.

We want to help youth gain a better sense of their decision-making abilities. They are in control, or "driving the bus," when it comes to actions. Their medication may be affecting how they *feel*, but no medication makes decisions. By using conversations that invite accountability, we also build strengths and empower youth.

Suggest Alternative Viewpoints That Fit the Same Evidence

Sometimes the stories youth have of themselves become so embedded in their lives that it becomes hard for them to see anything but the problems.

106 There's More Than One Way

When youth are in residential programs, a concern is that they may organize their views of themselves and others' views of them around the concept of mental illness. Pathologized youth behave pathologically. The job of the RYCW is to help such youth and those involved with youth to change their views and therefore both see and experience themselves as capable and accountable (Bertolino & O'Hanlon, 2002).

Because pathological views can remain with youth, we have to be patient. Exceptions are always present but sometimes will take longer to "stick." There are "aha moments" when youth or supportive others realize that they have overlooked some part of the equation. At other times simply identifying exceptions will not be enough. The exception itself will not be compelling enough to change a long-held story or belief. RYCWs exercise patience, understanding that we assemble our views of the world over time. Meaningful situations can happen at any time, but their influence may not be seen in the moment.

A key way to help youth and supportive others to change their views over time is to suggest an alternative viewpoint that still fits the same evidence that a youth is using to evaluate herself or a situation. We offer benevolent interpretations of situations, which is also known as "reframing." This involves casting a situation in a different light.

Important to this method is the use of conjecture or curiosity. Conjecture involves phrasing that allows ideas to be offered without imposing them. This is typically done by beginning comments with "I was curious" or "I wonder." Here's what combining conjecture with interpretation might look like:

YOUTH: I want to meet more people, but it's hard because I'll be living here [transitional living program] until I'm 18 and on my own. So I want to meet more people at school. You know, get involved more through school stuff. I thought about sports, but I'm no good at them. And I don't really even like sports. I mean I don't mind watching sports with friends, but I don't like playing. I'm a klutz and just look stupid playing. I just wish I could fit in. I want to be more involved than just hanging out and watching. And there is no way I am going to be a cheerleader. No way. How am I supposed to fit in?

RYCW: As I'm listening to you, I'm thinking about how much I admire you. You've really put thought into this. And I can hear how puzzling it seems. Sports is one way to get more involved. So here is what I am wondering: Maybe it is actually helpful to rule out playing sports. That way you're not wasting time on something that really doesn't interest you. By knowing what doesn't interest you, it creates an opportunity.

YOUTH: Huh? An opportunity?

RYCW: Exactly. The time that you might have spent doing something— like learning and participating in a sport that doesn't really interest you—you can now invest in something else. I am curious, you've said before that you wanted to learn an instrument. What about the possibility of learning an instrument and trying out for the marching band? Or, teams always need managers . . .

YOUTH: Oh, wow, I was totally not thinking about it that way. We have a school newspaper, and they do stories on sports and our theater club and . . . [smiles and pauses, seeming to think]. Wow! I do have some time to put into something else.

By exploring alternative viewpoints, we engage youth in opportunities to explore different possibilities. We are not seeking answers. Meaningful exchanges can pique curiosity from which new stories of hope and possibility may emerge. Should this tack prove unproductive, like others, we remain patient and search for other ways to help change their views. We are also careful with interpretations. As with other conversations, if youth feel we are giving short shrift to their emotions or views, they are likely to shut down. For this reason, it is important to employ ways to monitor the alliance as a means of gauging how direct or indirect the introduction of an alternative story ought to be.

If youth change their frames of reference, their actions are more likely to be in accord with those views. For instance, if the teenager in the previous case example sees not playing sports as an *opportunity* to pursue other interests and her view changes, a change in her actions will likely follow as well. As a result she might explore new options in accordance with her new view.

Envision It: Creating Compelling Futures

Throughout this book a central theme has been a focus on the future. This is because research indicates that having a vision of the future can affect what one does in the present. This is especially true for youth who, despite what some believe, very often have complex representations of the future and, in particular, purpose (Hill, Burrow, O'Dell, & Thornton, 2010). In this segment we develop this point further through two methods: *expectancy-talk* and *future pull.*

The primary way that RYCWs facilitate change is by engaging youth in strengths-based conversations. Over the course of this book, we have explored different ways of using language as a vehicle for change. Here we learn three additional methods for moving from problems to possibilities. A benefit of these methods is that they can be used at any point during interactions with youth. In fact, RYCWs will often report that these possibility-laced strategies become automatic over time. In other words, RYCWs don't have to think deliberately about using them—they occur spontaneously in conversations. For now, it is suggested that you practice these methods to become more comfortable with them.

The methods in this section are a form of "moving walkway" (O'Hanlon & Bertolino, 1998). Just as airports contain moving conveyor

108   *There's More Than One Way*

belts that take people to their destinations, language can do the same. When youth and supportive others come to us with stories that lack possibilities, we use our words as a conveyor belt to create compelling visions of the future, without youth or others having to exert any additional effort. Here is how we do this:

Expectancy-Talk

Assume the possibility of youth and/or supportive others finding solutions by using words and phrases such as "yet" and "so far." This kind of language presupposes that at some point in the near future things will change. This small shift in language can help to create a "light at the end of the tunnel."

Example 1   YOUTH: I'll never be good anything.
RYCW: So far you haven't attained the level of skill you'd like.
Example 2   YOUTH: I'm always in trouble.
RYCW: You haven't found a way to stay out of trouble yet.
Example 3   YOUTH: I don't have a future. Why should I even try?
RYCW: Up to this point you haven't found evidence that your future will be any different.

Turn Problems Into Goals

Recast the problem statement into a statement about a preferred future or goal.

Example 1   YOUTH: I'll never be able to get out of the gang.
RYCW: So you'd like to find a way to get out of the gang?
Example 2   YOUTH: No one cares what happens to me.
RYCW: You'd like to know that people care about you?
Example 3   YOUTH: I've been in trouble all my life.
RYCW: So one of the things that we could do here is to help you find a way to change your relationship with trouble?

Use Presupposition

Presuppose that changes and progress toward goals will occur by using words such as "when" and "will."

Example 1   YOUTH: No one wants to hang out with me because all I do is get in trouble.
RYCW: When you start to make friends, what will be different for you?
Example 2   YOUTH: I can't stop. I can't have fun unless I'm drinking.
RYCW: When you've put drinking behind you, what will you be doing instead?

Example 3 YOUTH: Everyone has the wrong idea about me.

RYCW: When people know you better, what will be different in your life?

The methods in this section are intended to be subtle. We are not trying to force-feed possibilities. As with all the methods in this book, we are opening up possibilities through *invitations*. Small openings can lead to bigger changes if we exercise patience. A core task of the RYCW is to become comfortable with new ways of using language. Just as language can restrict, confine, confuse, and limit, it can open, encourage, clarify, and empower.

Future Pull: Finding a Vision for the Future

The following three-step process can help youth better describe their preferred futures—what they want for themselves and supportive others. One of the reasons this method is compelling is because it presents an alternative to the idea that what happens to youth in the future is determined by the past. We suggest, instead, that youth can be pulled toward their futures—which begins with a vision. We want to encourage youth to dream of what is possible and then identify ways of achieving at least some variation of that vision. Success in this regard is not measured in "either/or" terms but rather that youth took some steps in the direction of what they hope for themselves.

The first step is to *find a vision of the preferred future* through one or more the questions that follow:

- What do you think is important for you to accomplish during your youth or teenage years?
- What is your vision of a good future?
- What dreams did you or do you have for yourself in upcoming days/weeks/months/years?
- What are you here on the planet for?
- What in your view are teenagers/young people meant to accomplish before becoming adults?
- What is an area in which you think you could make a contribution?
- What would you try to do with your life if you knew you could not fail?

A second step involves *dealing with dissolving perceived barriers to the preferred future*. Sometimes youth are clear about how they want things to be in the future but perceive barriers and may have a fear of failure. They may think they are inadequate to the task of making their dreams happen or think there must be an element of certainty before they are willing to commit. Next are questions to assist with this second part of the three-step process:

- What do you see as getting in the way of where you want to be in your life?

110 *There's More Than One Way*

- What do you see as stopping you from realizing your dream or vision?
- What do you believe must happen before you can pursue your dreams or vision?
- What actions haven't you taken to make your dream or vision come true?
- What things stand in the way of the future you want for yourself?
- What would your heroes, role models, or people you admire do, if they were you, to make this dream or vision happen?
- What are you thinking or doing that they wouldn't?

The third and final step of future pull is *making an action plan to reach the preferred future*. Making a plan helps youth identify specific things that can be done as opposed to leaving their dream or vision as just a thought. Here are some ideas for questions to help with this aspect:

- What could you do in the near future that would represent steps toward your future?
- What would be a first step?
- What will you do as soon as you leave here that will help you move just a little closer toward your dream or vision?
- What will you be thinking that will help you take that step?

With most youth just getting them to gaze from the past to the future will be a major reorientation. And this reorientation will give RYCWs a better idea of how youth see their futures and will provide information that can help determine directions for services. Again, patience is very important as youth in residential programs very often envision their futures as bleak or as absent altogether. Our focus is straightforward—restore hope and a purpose to life.

The strategies described in the first part of this chapter are just a start. If you are interested in further options, please refer to the companion edition, *Thriving on the Front Lines*, which delves into methods both within and outside of residential settings.

Pathway 2: Changing Actions and Interactions

Just as the views that youth and others hold can be problematic, so can their actions and interactions, what they *do*. The dilemma with actions and interactions is that they become patterned, repeating over and over unless interrupted in some way. It's as if youth become frozen in their behaviors—stuck in a moment they can't get out of. In this last section of Chapter 5, we explore a variety of ways to help youth and supportive others change problem patterns.

One of the ways to understand patterns is by thinking about how an actor would learn to play a role in a movie. The actor would study the

There's More Than One Way 111

mannerisms, habits, routines, and so on to gain as accurate a depiction as possible. The psychiatrist Milton Erickson often asked his patients, "If I were you, how would I do your problem?" Erickson knew that if he could understand the patterns in behavior, particularly the ones that were troublesome, he could find at least one point to intervene. This very idea is helpful to RYCWs because to change patterns, we typically only need to make a small change.

The identification of patterns begins with curiosity. We keenly observe youth in an effort to notice patterns that help and those that hinder. We keep in mind that the very essence of patterns is that they repeat. So we ask: What kinds of actions do youth take or how do they interact with others in ways that interfere with everyday life? This point is rather important because some patterns that may appear problematic to RYCWs do not seem that way to youth.

A colleague and I described the process of identifying problematic patterns this way:

> We explore with clients the negative problem patterns that seem to be inhibiting and intruding in their lives. We seek to be geographers, exploring the topography and coastline of Problem-Land. We want to know the details of the problem or symptom, and help the client to find ways of escaping it. (O'Hanlon & Bertolino, 1998, p. 66)

To ferret out the patterns that surround and maintain problems, we explore the following areas:

- How specifically is the pattern a problem?
- What is the frequency [rate] of the problem? How often does it typically happen [once an hour, once a day, once a week]?
- What is the typical timing [time of day/week/month/year] of the problem?
- What is the usual duration of the problem? How long does it typically last?
- What is the range of the problem's intensity?
- Where [location and spatial patterns] does the problem typically happen?
- Who else is involved? What do others who are around or involved usually do when the problem is happening?

We again rely on action-talk to bring clarity to the description of problems. We want to be as clear as possible about the frequency, rate, timing, duration, and so on. We do not need to know everything about problem sequences, just enough to be helpful. As we have learned, ambiguous, vague depictions of problems can contribute to confusion and misdirected attempts to intervene. Then, with informational details about the

112   *There's More Than One Way*

problem, we can begin to explore ways of changing some aspect of the problem sequence. There are two primary ways to change action and interactional patterns: depatterning and repatterning. There is also a third pathway that involves exercises for increasing happiness and well-being as described in the companion text, *Thriving on the Front Lines*.

Method 1: Depatterning

A first way of changing patterns is *depatterning*. We find some place to *alter the repetitive pattern*. By altering we mean interrupting, disrupting, modifying, or changing patterns. This method offers a multitude of options to RYCWs because of the many places available to intervene. In addition, several methods can be combined together as needed, bringing forth even more possibilities.

At this point there is a very important consideration to be made about the methods that follow. To illustrate each method, case illustrations will be used. Some of these illustrations may appear superficial, short-sighted, and possibly even insensitive. First, all the examples are real. Only names have been changed. Second, and more to the point, in all the examples, the youth were treated with respect, and safety was always at the forefront. Methods should never put the safety of youth at risk. To this end, the process of changing patterns that are pervasive and intrusive is challenging work. And in each situation, there was follow-up to the intervention. In most cases staff worked collectively to help the youth portrayed find a different method of expression.

Let's now consider several ways to alter problematic patterns. Each example will be illustrated through a case example.

Change the Duration of the Problem

Xavier, an 11-year-old, would refuse to go to bed at "lights out." The youth would say, "You can't make me go to bed. Just try and see what happens." When a RYCW on shift would turn out the lights, Xavier would turn them back on. He would also pace around the room and bark like a dog, which would interfere with his roommates' ability to get to sleep. The pattern would continue for about 10–15 minutes until a RYCW would have to separate him from other youth by having him leave the bedroom. The problem was contributing to increased hostility between Xavier and other male residents, who reported being "tired of the same crap every night."

Having studied the pattern, a RYCW decided to lengthen the duration of the problem. Just before lights out, the RYCW approached Xavier and said, "From now on, I am going to need you to refuse to go to bed for at least 20 minutes." Xavier seemed puzzled by the RYCW's statement and continued his bedtime pattern. The RYCW sat on a chair in the bedroom (which also had three other male youth in it), with the lights on, and stared at his watch, counting every minute. Initially, Xavier danced around the room and make barking noises. A few of the youth at first appeared bothered, then pulled the covers over their heads and ignored him. At 12 minutes Xavier lay down on his bed. The RYCW waited until a full 20 minutes passed and then left. The next night, a different RYCW gave the same directive to Xavier just before lights out, then pulled up a chair and began counting. After 3 minutes, Xavier said, "Can we just stop now? I'm too tired for this." The RYCW agreed. The problem was resolved.

Change the Time (of Day, Week, Month, or Year) of the Problem

A 14-year-old by the name of Laurie would throw "temper tantrums" on days when a recreational activity was chosen that that she did not like. Her tantrums would involve stomping her feet, yelling obscenities, and then sitting in the floor and refusing to go on the outing. Her pattern was consistent, although every once in a while she would reply to staff's attempts at communicating by saying, "Blah, blah, blah."

An interesting aspect of Laurie's behavior was that pattern would occur between 3 and 3:30 in the afternoon, which was the time when residents were informed of the afternoon's activity. Since activities began at 4, there wasn't much time to regroup and get ready when Laurie would go into her pattern. In this way her behavior was interfering with other youth participating in the activities.

The RYCWs on shift decided to change the time of the pattern around the problem. Instead of waiting until 3 or later to tell the group of the activity, they pulled Laurie aside at 2:30. They said, "We are going to do an activity that we think you will really enjoy. It's also one that you did not want to do last week. So we are telling you early so you will have plenty of time to let out your feelings." Laurie stared at the RYCW but did not say anything. Then the RYCW said, "We are going to the park. Okay, time to let it out." Laurie frowned and let out a deep sigh. The RYCW said, "We've got lots of time. It's only 2:33. Would you like to maybe express yourself more?" Laurie walked out of the room. Staff continued to tell her of activities early to interrupt the timing of the problem.

Change the Sequence (Order) of Events

Each day, Evan, a 12-year-old, would return to the emergency shelter from the off-site school and say, "I am not doing my chores!" Sometimes she would change her mind on her own and end up doing them, but more often than not she would persist with her refusal. Staff had explored the differences between times that she changed her mind versus times she did not to no avail. The problem had evolved to the point that several of the RYCWs were growing increasingly frustrated with the "power struggles" that occasionally ensued. And it seemed that even if an intervention worked one day,

114   *There's More Than One Way*

it would fall flat the next. Staff wanted to avoid using consequences with the issue, and yet they felt they were running out of options.

In a staffing a RYCW commented that there did seem to be a pattern of staff waiting to see how Evan would act after school—hoping for the best—even though her pattern was consistent. After further discussion, a RYCW who was due to be on shift when Evan got home from school came up with the idea of changing the pattern by "beating her to the punch." That afternoon, as soon as Evan returned, the RYCW met her at the door and said, "Good to see you, Evan. Do you want to refuse to do your chore right now or in five minutes?" Evan gave the RYCW a strange look and replied, "What?" She then walked away. The same RYCW approached her again 5 minutes later and said, "What about now? Do you want to refuse to do your chore now or in maybe two more minutes?" After a third time, Evan went into the staff office and said, "You guys are acting weird. I just want to get my chore over with."

Interrupt or Otherwise Prevent the Problem

A group of three youths would routinely create disturbances at bedtime and refuse to quiet down. One evening, a RYCW told the three boys, "Since you all seem to be so alert at bedtime, I'm going to give you the opportunity to use that alertness to learn something new. There's no reason to waste all that energy!" The RYCW then brought the three boys to the kitchen and began to read stories from the newspaper. When they began to doze off, the RYCW would raise his voice and show exuberance regarding the story being read. When they asked to go to bed, he said, "Already? We're just getting started!" The problem was interrupted, and we did not have any further problems at bedtime.

Add a New Element to the Problem

Chase was an 11-year-old who would scream expletives around the house and then deny that he had done so. It was decided during staffing that the RYCWs on duty would each carry pocket-sized audio recorders and turn them on when Chase began his verbal escapades. Chase was informed that this was the plan. The RYCWs never had to use the recorders. By adding a new element to the problem sequence, the pattern had changed.

Break Up a Problem Into Smaller Ones

During community meetings two particularly competitive youth would square off and argue. Since these arguments tended to disrupt the group meetings, a RYCW brought in a cooking timer and set it for 2 minutes. Then one youth was told he had 2 minutes to give his point of view. Once the timer went off, it was the other youth's turn. They were only to argue one point at a time, and if others wanted to be part of the discussion, they

There's More Than One Way 115

would also be given 2 minutes. By arguing just one point at a time, they were able to break their larger conflict into smaller, specific points.

*Reverse the Direction in the Performance
of the Problem (Paradox)*

A 15-year-old, Jade, would disagree with RYCWs sometimes because she had a difference of opinion but more often just for the sake of being disagreeable. Many of her arguments made little sense, and as a result several RYCWs were becoming frustrated with Jade, feeling that "everything" was a debate with her. As a result conversations between the RYCWs and Jade were growing increasingly strained. Then a RYCW decided it might be worthwhile to encourage Jade's disagreements. The RYCW said, "Jade, we're going to work with you so you can make better arguments. Otherwise there's no point in arguing." Jade did not want to learn to argue better. She replied, "That's stupid." The RYCW countered, "Saying it's stupid is not a good argument. We'll work on that." Jade walked away.

The next day Jade begin arguing a point with a RYCW. Instead of arguing back, the RYCW grabbed a pen and pad of paper and began taking notes, critiquing Jade's argument. When Jade stopped to try and figure out what was going on, the RYCW said, "Please continue. And if you could use more emotion, that would help. Really get into it!" Jade shook her head and walked away. The problematic pattern was changing by having Jade *do more of the problem*, which, in effect, took the spontaneity out of it.

From a collaborative, strengths-based approach, RYCWs are not trying to be experts. Instead they strive for creativity and spontaneity, injecting humor into situations that often involve annoying patterns. When it comes to changing patterns, there are no recipes or step-by-step, tried-and-true methods. What is required of RYCWs is a personal philosophy in which relationships are valued and patience and hope are part of every interaction and shift. Let's now explore another overarching method for changing patterns of action and interaction.

Method 2: Repatterning

A second global way of changing problematic patterns is *repatterning*, in which we *identify and encourage solution patterns*. The method differs from depatterning in that instead of altering existing patterns, we are looking to identify, evoke, and apply already existing strengths, abilities, and resources. We are not trying to convince youth and supportive others of these existing solution patterns and of their strengths. We don't say, "You can do it! Just look at all your strengths!" Doing so can be invalidating. Instead, we use historical examples of what youth and supportive others have already done as evidence of their strengths. To do this we say,

116 *There's More Than One Way*

"How were you able to do that?" or "What kind of person are you that you were able to [past example]?"

We continue to acknowledge the experience of youth and supportive others as we explore, as would Sherlock Holmes, aspects that run counter to problem patterns. Through questioning, we work to evoke some sense of competence and experience solving problems that youth already possess. But because youth may struggle recalling times when things were different, including what they did in those situations, we use various methods to identify and build on those solution patterns. Next are several ways to do this.

Find Out About Previous Solutions, Including Partial Solutions and Successes

Even when situations appear stuck, there are times when the problem hasn't come on full force. In other cases, a youth or supportive other expected the problem and it didn't happen at all. These exceptions are opportunities to build on partial successes and solutions. What follows are examples of questions that can assist with finding out about previous solutions.

- Tell me about a time when things didn't go the way you wanted and you got upset, yet you were able to get somewhat of a handle on the situation. What was different about that time or those times?
- You've taken off from home five out of the last seven nights. How did you keep yourself from taking off the other two nights?
- You mentioned that you usually lose your temper and scream when you get mad, but yesterday you didn't do those two things even though you said you were very mad. How did you do that?
- Tell me about a time when you didn't want to do your chores but you decided to anyway. How did you make that decision?

Action descriptions are again front and center when finding out what youth are doing or have done differently? We are also *presupposing* that there have been times when things were better. We are not asking *if* there have been times. We know there have been times when things have been different and are inquiring what happened, when it happened, and how it happened.

Let's take the example of the youth who typically screams when he loses his temper and is mad. Here's how a RYCW might talk with the youth to evoke a solution pattern:

RYCW: On a few previous occasions, you've lost your temper and screamed when you've gotten mad, but you didn't last night. How did you do keep a little calmer?

YOUTH: I don't know. I just did.

There's More Than One Way   117

RYCW: Take your time. Something was different—maybe just slightly . . .
YOUTH: I just told myself no.
RYCW: You told yourself no. And then what happened when you told yourself that?
YOUTH: I calmed down.
RYCW: Right, you did. And that's what was different because usually you would have screamed. Then how did you actually calm down?
YOUTH: I just kept saying to myself, "Don't do it. Don't get in trouble." Then I went and watched TV with Ed and Shane.
RYCW: So you said a couple things to yourself. First you said no to yourself, then, "Don't do it. Don't get in trouble." You then put those words to work by following them. You left the scene and went to watch TV with Ed and Shane.
YOUTH: Yeah. That's what I did.

Sometimes youth will have a hard time describing what they did differently. In these instances, we can offer multiple-choice options. Staying with the same example, if things had not opened up, we might have said, "So did you find yourself thinking differently?" or "Did you step away from the situation that was making you mad?" or "Maybe it was something else, something altogether unique about this situation." Multiple-choice inquisitions will often lead to clarification because youth will agree, disagree, or modify what we have offered into the equation. Sometimes youth will even say, "No, actually what I did was _____." Even if youth say little else, at minimum follow-up questions will lead to reflection, which is how learning takes place.

When exploring solution patterns, we keep in mind that for many youth, it will be too much to ask, "Tell me about a times when you didn't have the problem." It is better to inquire about small indicators of success. A RYCW might say, "Tell me about a time when things went a little bit better." Smaller increments or shades of difference will usually be easier to identify (Bertolino, 2014).

Should a youth remain persistent that a particular problem is never any better, we do two things. First, we make sure to acknowledge and validate the youth's experience. Second, we work backward from worst to best. Here's an example of how to do this:

RYCW: You mentioned that you argue a lot with your mom on the phone. Tell me about a time recently when you argued a bit less.
YOUTH: Never. We always argue when we talk on the phone.
RYCW: Okay. So it seems to you that in the past when you've talked with your mom on the phone, you've argued. And you've already told me that you talk with her each day. So which day this week was the worst?
YOUTH: That's easy. It was Friday.
RYCW: What happened?

118 *There's More Than One Way*

YOUTH: She really screamed at me—for nothing. I didn't do shit.

RYCW: I'm sorry that happened to you. That must have been tough.

YOUTH: A little. But I'm used to it.

RYCW: You are used to it, but it doesn't make it any easier. And what you said about Friday made me curious. If Friday was the worst recent day, what was Wednesday like, or maybe even Thursday or Saturday? They may have been bad but not as bad as Friday.

YOUTH: She still yelled but not as much.

RYCW: What do you think that was all about?

YOUTH: I guess it was because we talked before she started drinking.

We acknowledge and validate while simultaneously scanning for any evidence of a solution pattern that can be imported into the present situation. As detailed throughout this book, it's generally more helpful to use "solution-talk" rather than "problem-talk." For instance, if a RYCW were using problem-talk, he or she might say, "Tell me about a time when [the problem] wasn't quite as bad." Using solution-talk, the statement would instead be, "Tell me about a time when things were just a little better or more manageable with [the problem]." The idea is that solution-talk can orient youth and supportive others toward what's working. However, as illustrated earlier, RYCWs will sometimes need to adjust because a youth does not relate to such a focus. RYCWs can do just as well at eliciting and evoking solution patterns by talking about problems.

Find Out What Happens When the Problem Ends or Starts to End

Problems have end points. Even if end points are temporary or short-lived, *they still are end points.* And because there are end points, there are corresponding solution patterns. By exploring the details around how problems come to an end or temporarily pause, we can learn about ways of changing problem patterns. Here are some questions to help with identifying sequences involved with problem end points:

- How do you know when [the problem] is beginning to wind down or come to an end? What's the first thing you notice?
- How might others be able to tell when [the problem] is letting up or starting to subside just a little?
- What do others do that helps to bring [the problem] to an end?
- What have you noticed helps you personally wind down when a situation has been bad and maybe even gotten out of hand? What is your "reset" button?

The following case example illustrates how a solution pattern can be extracted by finding out how a problem comes to an end.

There's More Than One Way   119

Shannon had been in the emergency shelter for 2 days. She had avoided talking with other youth in the program even though they tried to engage her. On each shift the RYCWs would encourage Shannon to "mingle," but it seemed the more they tried the more Shannon withdrew. On her third day, a RYCW noticed Shannon smiling as another youth talked with her. Shannon was not observed saying anything, but she was communicating nonverbally. Later that same day, Shannon spontaneously spoke up during a community meeting. By the evening she was observed talking freely with other youth. That was on a Monday. Tuesday, Shannon was again withdrawn.

Emily, a RYCW, sat down with Shannon and asked her what had changed between Monday evening and Tuesday morning. Shannon shrugged her shoulders as if to say, "I don't know" or "I don't want to say." Emily then shared some collective observations of staff. "We've seen you go through some ups and downs in just the few days you've been here. I was hoping you might be able to help us to better understand how we can help you, but first we want to make sure what we have seen in accurate. Would it be okay if I shared with you what we have seen?" Shannon shook her head yes.

Emily then described how staff had seen Shannon keep to herself and, seemingly, be deliberate in trying to avoid others at times. Emily wondered aloud if Shannon might have something weighing heavily on her mind, if she took some time to get to know others, or if it were something else altogether. Because Shannon was silent, Emily used a smorgasbord of options to see if she was "warm" or "cold" with her guesses. Then Emily spoke about how staff had noticed Shannon starting to gradually connect, first by smiling and being physically closer to other youth in the program, then by engaging them in conversation.

As Emily spoke, Shannon moved from staring at the floor to periodically glancing at Emily to making consistent eye contact. It was as if the pattern of gradually becoming engaged with others—the pattern that had taken place over a few days—was now taking place over the course of a few minutes. Emily said to Shannon, "Something seems to happen, and I'm not sure I quite get it. So anything you would be willing to share would really help." The RYCW then went on to meticulously describe the pattern staff had observed of Shannon being disengaged, then engaged, then disengaged again. This seemed to stir something within Shannon because she started to talk about the pattern. The conversation ensued:

SHANNON: I have times when I feel really alone. Like I can't relate to what other people are saying. I don't want to be around other people, and I really don't want to talk.
EMILY: That sounds really hard. I'm sorry you feel so alone at times. What helps you feel a little better?

120 *There's More Than One Way*

SHANNON: I'm not really sure.

EMILY: Okay, what do you notice about when you start to gradually move from feeling alone to feeling more connected to others, even if it's just a for a little while?

SHANNON: Well, I know if I just keep thinking about the same stuff over and over, it gets worse. But sometimes what breaks me out of it is another person talking calmly to me—just like you did here. And that's what Kim did Monday. When that happens it feels like the weight is lifting off my shoulders. I feel light and happy.

EMILY: Wow. That's a great description. Then what happens?

SHANNON: Then I'm out of it. I can smile and laugh and talk. I don't worry about things as much. I mean, everything doesn't go away, I just feel like I can handle things.

EMILY: And what is in place of feeling alone?

SHANNON: Being connected to others.

EMILY: So when the feeling of being alone is lifting and is being replaced by feeling connected to others, that signals the end of the sequence for you?

SHANNON: Yeah, but just for a little bit, then it comes back.

EMILY: I think I understand. And let's see if we can help with the feeling of being connected to others last longer. But first we want to shorten the time that you feel alone by helping you connect to others much quicker . . .

SHANNON: I really need that.

EMILY: Got it. So will it help for staff to use calm voices to invite you into more connection?

SHANNON: That will help, and so will telling jokes and making me laugh.

EMILY: That's very helpful. What else helps to shut down that feeling of aloneness and increase your connection to others?

SHANNON: Just including me in things and not shying away just because I may not be talking.

EMILY: Thank you, Shannon.

By continuing this conversation, it is likely that even more information about how the problem ends or starts to end could be gleaned, which could then be used to help Shannon feel more connected to others. Again, it is not a cure we are seeking. We are pursuing greater well-being. When RYCWs begin to think in terms of cures and fixes, trouble ensues. We aim for growth through change.

Search for Contexts of Competence

Even though youth may be experiencing problems in specific areas of their lives, there are often competencies, abilities, and solution patterns elsewhere that can be helpful with the problem at hand. We call these

There's More Than One Way 121

abilities in other areas of youth's lives *contexts of competence.* To identify these competences, we inquire about jobs, hobbies, sports, interests, or areas of knowledge or skills youth have that can be tapped into to help with problems of focus while in our residential programs.

Contexts of competence involve exceptions. We want to transfer abilities from one context to another, which means first identifying those abilities and when and how they were used. To get started it can be helpful to return to initial interviews and information-gathering processes to search for abilities that came up in discussions about school, employment, family, other relationships, and so on.

Let's consider an example of how to identify and transfer a competency from one context to another with a 17-year-old:

RYCW: How have things been going?

YOUTH: My teacher thinks I am going to keep getting into fights. I just had one. The other one wasn't really a fight. I just pushed Joe because he pushed me first. Now they are talking about putting me in another school.

RYCW: Your teachers are concerned about you getting into fights so much so that they're talking about moving you to another school.

YOUTH: Yeah. But those kids say stuff to me. They call me "retarded" and "stupid." If they would shut up, there wouldn't be a problem.

RYCW: I can see how that might get to you. And it's not right for others to say stuff like that.

YOUTH: It's not. I don't call other people names.

RYCW: I've heard that you are respectful in that way. And that has me curious about something.

YOUTH: What is it?

RYCW: Well, it may be something little. I'm not sure. I just keep thinking about it. You have now been in our program for three weeks, right?

YOUTH: Yeah, three weeks.

RYCW: And you haven't had any fights here? Am I wrong about that?

YOUTH: I haven't been in any trouble here. None!

RYCW: That is really impressive. How have you done that even though we have kids here who do say disrespectful things from time to time?

YOUTH: I stay focused. I need to be here so I can get my life together.

RCYW: How do you stay focused?

YOUTH: I think about living in an apartment as soon as I am 18. I think about getting a job and a car. If I get kicked out of here, those things will be out of reach.

RYCW: That all makes sense. And when disrespectful comments are thrown at you, you think about those things?

YOUTH: Yeah.

RYCW: So you have this ability to stay focused on what is important to you when you are here. And that is an excellent skill. It will help you

122 *There's More Than One Way*

when you are on your own and have a job and a car. Now how can that same focus help you at school?

YOUTH: I hadn't really thought about it. I like my school, and if I get sent to another one or I let those dudes get under my skin, then it's going to be even harder to get to where I want.

RYCW: So what can you do while at school to maintain your focus on the future?

YOUTH: Can I have a copy of my goal sheet? I know it by heart, but if I put a copy in my notebook I can remind myself a bunch of times during the day.

RYCW: Sure, I'll get you a copy as soon as we are done.

YOUTH: I can even look at it before class ends because most of the trouble is in the hallways between classes.

Although youth in residential settings will sometimes be less involved in activities outside of the programs, they will still have abilities that can go unnoticed. The key is for RYCWs to explore areas outside of the immediate problem area. Not every skill will be transferable from one context to another, but identifying competencies serves as a starting point for finding this out. Once abilities are identified, we ask, "How could you use [competency] in dealing with [problem]?"

Find Out Why the Problem Isn't Worse

There have been a few instances in this book in which "why" questions have been encouraged. When it comes to the severity of problems, why questions can be helpful. In many cases, asking "Why aren't things worse?" will render youth silent. And, ironically, we aren't really interested in the "why." We are interested in youth pondering the question because it will more often than not be new to them. And with youth in a reflective mode, we can ask more important questions that can help with identifying solution patterns.

Often referred to as "coping-sequence questions," a focus on why things aren't worse serves two purposes (Bertolino, 2010; Selekman, 1997). First, it provides perspective for youth and supportive others when they really consider that they could be dead, incarcerated for life, and so on. It also brings to light that other people struggle, sometimes even more so. And second, it can yield information about what youth and supportive others have done to keep things from deteriorating even further. Here are some questions to assist with exploring this area further.

- Why aren't things worse with your situation?
- What have you done to keep things from getting worse?
- What steps have you taken to prevent things from going downhill any further?

There's More Than One Way 123

- What else has helped to keep things from getting worse?
- How has that made a difference with your situation?

The following case example illustrates how coping questions can help to identify a solution pattern with a 14-year-old youth.

Anita had been failing some of her classes at the public school she was attending through her residential program. (This is a common practice in some states.) One evening, a curious RYCW asked, "How come you haven't failed all of your classes?" Anita replied, "Some of my classes are easy." The RYCW persisted, "Yeah, but you still could have blown them off and not done anything at all, letting things bottom out. What specifically did you do in the classes you are passing?" "I do my work, silly. And I get to class on time. That's about it," Anita offered. The RYCW replied back, "That's great. You really have a good strategy for success and for keeping yourself from bottoming out. So how can you use your success with your other three classes—the ones that aren't going so well and could drag you your GPA down if you continue as is?" Anita thought about it before answering, "I am going to try harder. I don't like those three other classes, but I know I have to do them. So I am going to show up on time and start doing my work." The RYCW then explored with Anita ways that staff could act as a buffer—a way of stopping any downward movement before it happens. So Anita and staff agreed that staff would sit with Anita each night and talk about her success, including what went well, and her challenges and develop plans for directly addressing those challenges.

It will sound strange to some youth when they are asked about why things aren't worse. But once engaged in conversation, youth will typically learn more about their untapped abilities and just how resilient they truly are. And when youth become tuned into the combination of their abilities and resiliencies, their sense of hope can increase.

In this chapter we have explored two overarching pathways—changing views and changing actions and interaction—within which are many strategies for RYCWs to use to stimulate change. In the following chapter, we will delve into the issue of crisis in residential programs. What we have learned is that the most effective RYCWs use specific principles, practices, and strategies and that these characteristics are communicated among successful programs.

6 In the Moment
Strategies for Crisis Prevention

There is an unfortunate perception that surrounds residential programs. Programs serve youth 24 hours a day, 7 days a week, 365 days a year. Residential programs do not close. They do remarkable work, and few hear about it. And then, a single incident occurs and within a short time is on every news report. Staff will say, "It's not fair." It's not. But it is the work we do. Just as physicians and nurses take an oath to provide the best care possible, we do the same with the youth in our programs.

To this end, there will always be an element of unpredictability in residential programs. Still, there are many steps RYCWs can take and practices that can reduce the probability of incidents *and* help us continuously improve the quality of care. A first step is more philosophical than practical. That is, we strive to maintain confidence in our ability and that of our coworkers to handle whatever occurs, at any given time. We also prepare for scenarios that could put youth at risk and cast doubt on our ability to do the job. Practice and preparation matter. A second step is the actions we take to make our programs better.

In this chapter we consider two interrelated roads to crisis: prevention and intervention. In effect, prevention is an intervention and vice versa. When we do one, we are doing the other. To be effective in both realms, we maintain our sense of awareness of our setting, the youth, and the situations, thinking several steps ahead when possible. Thinking ahead is a form of reflection and behavioral rehearsal, which prepares us to respond as opposed to react. And finally, we balance intuition with supportive evidence by communicating with coworkers, checking out what our guts are telling us by getting feedback. There will of course be situations that occur spontaneously, with little or no time to plan, which is further reason to run through scenarios in our minds or, even better, with coworkers. Let's now consider different strategies for managing and preventing crisis.

Surveying the Territory

In an article for the *New Yorker*, Boston surgeon Atul Gawande (2004) tells about Cincinnati Children's Hospital's (CCH) work to improve the lifespan of persons with cystic fibrosis (CF). Although CCH is an excellent hospital, its outcomes with patients with CF were only average. Whereas patients treated at CCH were living on average to about 30 years old, at the top centers patients were living on average to about 46 years of age. That is an enormous difference, and CCH knew it. And they did something about it by studying what other health-care providers were doing to improve care of patients with CF. CCH was proactive.

A critical point of Dr. Gawande's article was the *costs of being average* in health care. In short, average physicians and hospitals have more complications, more postoperative infections, and, unfortunately, more loss of life. In contrast some physicians and hospitals have fewer problems and better outcomes. Now ask yourself: Would I want to see an average doctor?

Let's delve into this just a bit further. The bell curve is a statistical way of understanding how data is distributed. The "bell" represents the largest cluster of data in a normal distribution, with the midpoint being the average. Although there are arguments for and against the bell curve, in a very general way it helps identify a range in which most of the data will fall. The empirical rule is that "average" is typically between 68.26% and 95.44%, depending on whether we are using one or two standard deviations (SD) to the left and right of the mean. So if the outcomes of 100 residential programs were being studied, approximately 68% of those programs would be within +1 or –1 SD of the mean. Translated, 32% of programs would be considered as performing either better or worse than the 68% that cluster around the mean (average). Of that 32%, roughly 16% of programs would be considered exceptional and 16% would be considered very poor in terms of outcomes.

There is no shame in being average. Most programs are in fact average, but there are consequences. That's because youth in some programs do get better services and as a result have better outcomes (and, of course, some do worse). In residential programs our aim is not perfection. Just as CCH, we want to get better, and getting better takes work. There is good news. There are many very good residential programs from which much has been learned. One of the ways residential programs can get better is by understanding their collective strengths and areas of vulnerability. A starting point is to review policies and practices around how crises are prevented, prepared for, and managed. The territory must be surveyed and a plan put into place to achieve the program vision. Committees can also be formed for the purpose of investigating strengths and weaknesses.

Staffings and Team Meetings Revisited

In Chapter 4, staffings and team meetings were discussed. These forums are excellent for discussions on safety and the prevention of crises. Ironically, one of the things that is frequently overlooked when it comes to crises is what is working when things are calm and going better within a

126   *In the Moment*

program. By adding the topic of crisis prevention to team meetings, staff can focus attention on strengths including what has worked in situations that could have been worse, exceptions to patterned behavior, and when things have gone well, in general. Action-talk should be used so that strengths discussed are specific. Examples of questions that can help with identifying strengths and preventing crises include these:

- What are examples of things that happened on recent shifts that appeared to keep things calm, settled down, or peaceful?
- What situations were challenging but did not evolve beyond minor disruptions?
- What specific things were tried that seemed to help, even just a little, with potentially volatile or challenging situations?
- What was learned from situations that were challenging? How can what was learned be helpful in the future?

Group and Community Meetings

Another area of consideration is group or "community" meetings that occur with youth in residential programs on a daily or weekly basis. It is a good idea to run group meetings regularly so youth know they will have a format to share their feelings and thoughts outside of individual meetings. Group meetings can also be called if something has happened in a program that should be discussed right away. Examples might be an incident that involves the entire group, a change to a program, and so forth.

Group meetings provide opportunities for RYCWs to have conversations with youth about rules, current issues, concerns, and conflicts and to learn new skills. But group meetings are also a way for RYCWs to keep the pulse of a particular group of youth. RYCWs who are in tune to the vicissitudes of youth and encourage feedback are being proactive. By acknowledging frustration, worry, and other feelings youth may have, some of the emotional propensities of youth can be neutralized, thereby preventing the occurrence of crises. Here is an example of how a RYCW might begin a group or community meeting:

> This group is a chance for each of us to share what we think and feel about what goes on around here—in the program. You'll have a chance to talk about any concerns you might have. I also hope that you'll mention things that you think are going well. I've/we've also got a few things that I'd/we'd like to talk about, including things that are going well. Before we get going, let's agree to be respectful of one another. There are different ways of looking at things, and we want to be respectful of one another's thoughts and feelings. You don't have to agree with everything that is said here, just be respectful. This also means that there's no blaming here. If you have something

In the Moment 127

you want to say, speak about how it affects you and what you would like to see change. If you aren't sure how to word what you want to say, ask for help. Let's also agree to have just one person speak at a time. Each of you will have a chance to speak, if you choose to. This group is an opportunity for all of us to understand each other just a little better and to take a step forward in making your stay here as good an experience as possible, no matter the reason that brought you here.

In Chapter 3 we explored differences between pathology- and strengths-based conversations. Group meetings with youth are an excellent opportunity to put strengths-based conversations to work. For example, when a concern is raised, a RYCW will at some point ask for clarification to gain a clearer picture of that concern. From there the RYCW might also inquire as to what things might look like when things are better. Since there may be different views of the problem within a group, the RYCW will need to acknowledge and validate each youth and his or her view. Here's an example of how to do this:

RYCW: Who would like to talk about something that is on their mind?

PATRICK: I would. I'm pissed—really pissed off.

RYCW: Can you say more about it?

PATRICK: Some people should mind their own business!

RYCW: I'm not sure what you mean by that. Can you give an example?

PATRICK: Some people—some people in this room—say things behind other people's backs.

RYCW: Can you give an example, without naming names?

PATRICK: I told someone something about me that I didn't want anyone else to know, and it got blabbed all over.

DERRICK: I know you're not talking about me!

RYCW: Okay, this is clearly something that is upsetting to you, Patrick. And Derrick, you will have a chance to speak because it's important too. [Looks at Patrick] First, let me say that I am sorry that something you wanted to keep private was shared with others. What do you feel needs to happen so that you can begin to feel a little better about what's happened?

PATRICK: I don't know.

RYCW: Okay, you're not sure. How about if you give it some thought while I let others have the floor. [Looking to Derrick] Derrick, would you like to say something?

DERRICK: Well, I don't know if Patrick told anyone else but me, but I didn't rat him out. I don't do stuff like that.

RYCW: So you can understand why Patrick is upset.

DERRICK: Yeah, I understand. But I didn't say anything to nobody.

RYCW: Thank you, Derrick. Would anyone else like to speak?

128   *In the Moment*

KRISTEN: I don't know who said what or did what and I don't really care. People say stuff all the time, and it ain't right. I just don't want things to get worse because then this weekend is gonna suck. I came here because everyone at my home fights, and I can't handle any more of that.

RYCW: Thank you for speaking up, Kristen. I'm sorry things were so hard at home. And you're right. There's no room for fighting here—whether it's through words or actions. This place is here for you—all of you. So what are we going to do to get things back on track?

DERRICK: [Speaking to Patrick] Hey, man, I don't know who said what, but I'm your friend and want things to be cool between us.

PATRICK: [To Derrick] It's cool.

RYCW: [To the group] What I am hearing is that all of you want to move forward. And if this is resolved then that's great. If it's not, Patrick or Derrick or whoever, I really need you to talk with me after this or I can get another RYCW. We're in this together.

It's not that group meetings always end in clear resolution. If we can create forums for youth to talk about what's on their minds and try to mediate conflict toward some positive end, then we will have most likely accomplished enough to prevent further escalation. If, on the other hand, we choose to sit back and see what happens, the odds are far greater that problems will fester and get worse. Remember, hope is a catalyst for change, not a strategy. We must be active participants in the lives of youth and in relationships to create hope.

Sometimes group meetings can focus exclusively on group goals. In such cases there may be an overall group goal that is brought forth from the morning to the evening or from one day to the next. Group meetings can also be opportunities for each youth to develop and discuss a goal that was worked on during that day. Table 6.1, "A.M./P.M. Collective Goal Groups," is a form that might be used to discuss a collective group goal, and Table 6.2, "A.M./P.M. Individual Goal Groups," is a form that can be used with youth to set individual goals that are discussed in group sessions.

Questions that can be used in group meetings to facilitate conversation include these:

- What's been better with the group since the last unit/community meeting?
- What have you noticed happening that you would like to have continue with the group?
- What's one small change that might make things even better for all of you?
- Who here has made the most positive change since the last meeting?
- How does one, two, or even more of you doing better help the group too?
- What can help keep the momentum going?
- How can we, as staff, support you?

Table 6.1 A.M./P.M. Collective Goal Groups

A.M./P.M
Collective Goal Groups

A.M. Goal Group

Date: _____

Group Members Present: _____

_____

Group Leader: _____

Group Goal for Today: _____

1. How did the group decide on this goal?

2. On a scale of 1–10 (with 1 being a big problem and 10 being not much of a problem), how concerned is the group about the problem that led to this goal?

3. What will be signs that progress was made toward achieving this goal?

4. What strategies might be used during the day to work on this goal?

5. How might achieving this goal help the group as a whole?

P.M. Goal Group

Group Members Present: _____

_____

Group Leader: _____

1. On a scale of 1–10, how concerned is the group with the problem that led to the goal in the A.M. group?

2. What changes have been noticed that indicate that progress has been made toward the goal?

3. How has that progress benefited or helped the group as a whole?

4. What can each of you do after this group to move this goal forward just a little more?

Table 6.2 A.M./P.M. Individual Goal Groups

A.M./P.M.
Individual Goal Groups

A.M. Individual Goal Planning

Date: _____

Name of Youth: _____

Group Leader: _____

Goal for Today: _____

1. How did I decide on this goal?

2. On a scale of 1–10 (with 1 being a big problem and 10 being not much of a problem), how concerned am I about the problem that led to this goal?

3. What will be signs that progress was made toward achieving this goal?

4. What strategies might I use during the day to work on this goal?

5. How might achieving this goal help not just me but others as well?

P.M. Goal Follow-Up

Name of Youth: _____

Group Leader: _____

6. On a scale of 1–10, how concerned am I with the problem that led to the goal in the A.M. group?

7. What changes have been noticed that indicate that I made progress toward the goal?

8. How has that progress benefited me and helped the group as well?

9. What can I do after this group to move this goal forward just a little more?

In the Moment   131

Groups are rich with opportunities. We can work on individual goals or group goals, identify and mediate conflict, and so on. But perhaps one of the more underrated aspects of groups is that they can contribute to greater group cohesion, respect among members, and internal support. A result is more stability in programs. So, in effect, group meetings both serve as a preventative measure and as a form of intervention.

Strengths-Based Crisis Prevention and Intervention

In residential care there are many outdated practices that may have worked at one time or not at all, and yet they remain part of the territory. Today's RYCW must be more active, must be more persistent, and must be willing to step into unknown territory with a focus on doing things better. Without doubt one of the biggest challenges for RYCWs is crises. Seemingly out of nowhere, without reason, a youth becomes increasingly agitated and the RYCW is caught flat-footed. Or a caregiver and youth escalate into conflict and the RYCW does not feel prepared to respond. The thing is, crises do not occur randomly—there is always a reason and a context. But in the heat of the moment, seeking explanations is not an effective route. Rather, effective RYCWs *prepare to prevent* crises before they ever occur, and, when they do, they are also *prepared to respond.* Let's explore each.

Building Strengths Through Preparation

A colleague of mine, Charlie Appelstein (1998), speaks about "trouble-shooting in advance" by trying to stay several steps ahead of youth. Just as chess players see many moves when they look at a chessboard, we want to be prepared for as many moves as possible on the chessboard of residential services. To wit, the best intervention for dealing with crises is to prevent crises from ever happening. Prevention of crises requires several key ingredients: relationships, strengths, and hope. To begin, recall principle 2: *The therapeutic relationship makes substantial and consistent contributions to outcome.* The views youth hold of the relationship are the best process-related predictor of outcome; therefore, those who feel most connected to YFS staff and RYCWs, in particular, have fewer outbursts. This is because these youth feel safe and tend to have more evolved coping skills—a by-product of engaging in supportive relationships. Similarly, when these youth do escalate into crises, they are more likely to respond to attempts at de-escalation because of their relationships with RYCWs.

Second, there is a phrase, "Glance at problems, gaze at strengths." Awareness of the strengths of youth provides potential inroads to neutralize frustration, distress, and anxiety on the part of youth. Situations that might otherwise escalate can be avoided when RYCWs are aware of

132   *In the Moment*

exceptions that can be employed. Said differently, RYCWs who take the time to learn about youth *before crises occur* have more information to work with to short-circuit potential crises.

Third, crises frequently occur when there is an absence of hope. RYCWs can take measures to prevent crisis through environments and activities that increase youth's sense of hope and ability to cope more effectively when hope is diminished. For example, RYCWs might have youth practice relaxation, meditation, imagery, or yoga as ways of reducing anxiety and increasing happiness and well-being.

Crises are stressful. During times of intense stress, we tend to do and say things that are out of character. Words come out of our mouths that make us wonder where they came from. We are much more likely to become self-consumed and paranoid under stress. That's why we need crisis protocols. It is therefore important that crisis protocols are not only in place, but that they are routinely discussed and practiced. Furthermore, practice or run-throughs of protocols need to occur in conditions that emulate those likely to be experienced by staff (Ericsson, 2009). Practicing outside of such conditions does not create the same kind of stress. Role-plays are an excellent way to train in the use of crisis protocols.

When crises do occur, a consideration is that youth see no future—no point in "holding it together." When crises are triggered through conflict, youth can quickly move into a state of hyperarousal, affecting their ability to regulate emotion and think clearly. They are not, in the moment, able to evaluate the consequences that might result from their actions or the consequences assigned to them (e.g., loss of privileges, juvenile detention, etc.) as paling in comparison to the pain they are experiencing. When crisis is set in motion, RYCWs need to be prepared to respond, not react. Next we explore some ways to respond in the moment through brief interventions.

The best prepared RYCWs are aware of potential triggers for youth and what has worked to any degree in the past to keep situations from deteriorating further. For example, knowing that a youth responds well to a soft voice tone or better to females can be useful. Additionally, awareness of factors that might increase stress for youth can also be valuable. To this end, youth are not the only ones with triggers; knowledge of personal "hot buttons" serves as a form of personal preservation. This kind of self-knowledge is essential when things become intense. When RYCWs access their self-knowledge and do not take personally what youth do when in crisis, they are able to better respond to those situations.

Considerations for Crisis Management

As we have learned, relationships are created through best practices such as good listening and active listening. Through listening we learn *who youth are* through their stories and focus on their strengths and resources to help them to achieve their preferred futures. When crises do occur, there are considerations that RYCWs will want to be prepared to follow through on. Let's explore a few main points.

Safety First

First and foremost is the safety of those involved in the crisis. We want to ensure that the risk of harm to self or others is reduced as much as possible. When others are present around the youth in crisis, such as in residential programs or classrooms, it is important to reduce the audience by having those persons leave the area, minimally, and the room, if possible. Other professional staff can be helpful in these situations. We also want to exercise patience when it comes to safety. Pushing for the end of a crisis more often than not makes things worse. RYCWs who are patient and employ active listening skills will have more options than those who do not. That said, if a situation requires the support of law enforcement or emergency support to maintain safety, then appropriate actions should follow. However, RYCWs should avoid using any form of threats to de-escalate youth.

Maintain Awareness of One's Own Nonverbals

We all send nonverbal messages, more often than not unintentionally. Self-awareness around one's nonverbal behavior is essential to preventing a crisis from escalating to the point where someone gets hurt or, in worst cases, irreparable damage is done. Nonverbal behavior includes qualities such as physical posture, eye contact, voice tone, volume, and pace of speech. Specifically, we want to remain culturally sensitive to verbal phrases and tones and physical gestures and postures that might be misinterpreted and thus provoke further escalation. RYCWs can also use nonverbals as signals to help youth regain self-control. Examples include softer voice, slow rate of speech, and relaxed body posture or positioning.

Stick to Basic Information

RYCWs want to keep the questions to a minimum and not ask about things that matter little in crisis situations. Along these lines, we do not argue with youth. We do not want to throw fuel on a fire. For example, asking a youth why she gets angry when asked to do her homework or inquiring as to why a youth made "a big deal" about the choice of a meal being served is unhelpful. RYCWs should stick to information that will help resolve the issue at hand. This translates to identifying some minimal outcome. Most commonly the aim is a youth who is calmer and relaxed as evidenced by things such as slower breathing and rate of speech, relaxed posture, and statements that suggest improved insight and judgment.

134   *In the Moment*

Acknowledge and Validate

One of the most effective yet underutilized ways to de-escalate is through acknowledgment. As discussed in Chapter 3, acknowledgment and validation are a powerful combination. By acknowledgment we mean attending to what youth have communicated both verbally and nonverbally, letting them know that their experience, points of view, and actions have been heard and noted. To acknowledge we say, "Uh huh" or "I see." Validation involves letting youth know that whatever they are experiencing is valid. RYCWs can validate by using statements such as, "It's/That's okay" or "It's/That's all right." To combine acknowledgment with validation, add words or statements such as "It's/That's okay" or "It's all right" to what is being acknowledged. A RYCW using acknowledgment and validation might say, "It's okay to be pissed off" or "It's all right if you're pissed." It is crucial that RYCWs distinguish between internal experience and actions. Acknowledgment and validation are a form of permission for internal experience—how youth feel. We do not extend permission for actions that are harmful or destructive to self or others. We say, "It's okay to be so pissed you feel like hitting the wall. It's not okay to hit the wall."

Use Available Supports

There are times when a RYCW or other staff will struggle to reduce the tension of a situation. Knowing others who are on shift and/or available to help out can be instrumental. For peers who are present, consider handing off so another RYCW or staff can assist. Perhaps that person will have better rapport with the youth in crisis. Handoffs also provide opportunities to contact other support staff for consultation. One RYCW can seek consultation while the other talks with the youth in crisis. Conversely, handoffs can contribute to escalation, so be sure to let the youth know what is happening. For example, a RYCW might say, "Tracy is here now. Would it be okay if she talked with you and I stepped away?" In other cases there are staff who may be available by phone or are in a nearby office and can offer support. Because youth often respond to some staff better than others, keeping such options open can make a difference when situations are at a standstill. For instance, a RYCW might say, "Would you like me to call [name of staff] so you can talk with him/her?" It is advised to keep a short list of options for people to call otherwise a youth may become further frustrated when he or she is not able to call someone who is not approved. On-call supervisors are usually a good choice.

Strengths in Action: Methods for De-escalation

In this section we review a series of methods that serve as add-ons. These methods are add-ons in that they are intended to build on as opposed to

In the Moment 135

replace the considerations described in the previous section. As with all the methods detailed in this chapter and in Chapter 5, they are to be used with respect to the prior knowledge and culture of the youth.

Acknowledge and Presuppose Small Movements Forward

In the midst of crisis, very small movements or exceptions can translate to larger ones. For example, to a youth who pauses between bouts of screaming, a RYCW might say, "That's right. Everyone needs to take a breath every now and then. That was a very good breath. Maybe the next one can be even longer and more relaxing." First the movement is acknowledged, then there is the presupposition that the movement will continue in the future.

Cross-mirror

Whereas mirroring involves emulating another person's nonverbal behaviors such as posture, *cross-mirroring* is when a person mirrors another and then slowly introduces subtle changes. For example, with a youth who is talking rapidly, a RYCW may first join the pacing and then gradually begin to slow her rate of speech. Doing so can serve as a cue to relax and become calm. Next is an example:

I told a youth that I needed a few minutes to talk with him about an upcoming family meeting with his mother. He agreed but stated that he would not sit down in my office. As soon as he entered my office, he reiterated his point: "I'm not going to sit down. So don't tell me to. I'm going to just walk back and forth because that's what I want to do." I said, "I think you should do just that—keep on walking from one side of the office to another. Maybe from that brown chair you're next to over to the couch along the wall. And when you get to the couch you can turn around and head back toward the brown chair." I joined the young man's pattern, then began to direct it by specifying the pattern would be to walk between the chair and the couch. I then said, "And as you get to the brown chair, you can notice how comfortable it appears, and then turn around, and when you get to the couch, you can notice that the couch looks comfy too. As you walk back to the chair, you may be wondering which is more comfortable—the chair or the couch. And you don't have to sit down until you have decided which one appears most comfortable and until you're ready." The young man walked to the chair, paused, then turned and headed over to the couch, and paused a second time, just a bit longer. He then headed back to the chair, took a deep breath, and sat down. He then said, "I'm ready."

---

136 *In the Moment*

Go for What You Know

Knowing who youth are, including their interests, potential triggers, and exceptions to past crisis situations, can provide solutions in crisis situations. The first task is to invest in youth—to learn about what matters most to them, things that may set them off, and what has worked in the past. Of course, we cannot know all there is to know, but small investments of this sort frequently pay off. All that is required is time getting to know about youth. When in crisis, these tidbits can be used to neutralize tension. Here is an example:

> A youth had escalated to anger because another youth called him a name. Knowing the youth had a penchant for baseball, the RYCW said, "Eduardo, I remember you telling me how you learned to repeat funny lines from the movie *Major League* when umpires made calls you disagreed with during your games. Can you tell me one of those lines now?"

Offer Options

For some youth being in crisis means feeling trapped, without options. One way to help youth to feel more safe and in control is to offer options. A variation for offering options is known as "the illusion of alternatives" (Cade & O'Hanlon, 1993; O'Hanlon, 1987). This method involves offering options that lead to the same outcome. In other words, the options are limited but provide youth with a sense of choice. For example, a youth in crisis might be asked, "Do you want to talk with me or Jane?" Of course, the youth may refuse either option, but in many cases having an option will help. Let's see how to do this through an example:

> A youth in one of our residential facilities was threatening to hurt herself. When I arrived she was sitting in the corner of her room, refusing to go with the two paramedics who had been called to take her to the hospital. She had threatened to hit them if they approached her. I talked with her for a few minutes, but she did not say anything in return. So I said, "Maybe you would like to take a minute or two to get your thoughts together. Sometimes we just need time to clear our heads and then the answers are more obvious. Then, when you're ready—and not a moment before that—you can get up and go with the two gentlemen standing in the doorway. You may decide to go with them in 1 minute or 3 minutes or maybe even 5 minutes. It's entirely up to you." After about 2 minutes, the youth grabbed her pillow, got up, and went with the paramedics.

In the previous example, the youth was given different options—the most important of which was when to go with the "gentlemen." (This was deliberate. I was aware that due to her prior history of hospitalization, she was more likely to go with two men than two paramedics.) She was not given a choice of going, but when to go. That was enough for her to make a decision.

Provide Opportunities for Youth to "Save Face"

Perhaps one of the most effective ways to help youth de-escalate is by providing opportunities to save face. This means creating "outs" for youth. For example, it can be helpful to say, "You probably already thought of this _____ (fill in the blank)" or "This probably won't be a new idea to you, but I'll say what you already know, which is that _____ (fill in the blank)." The point is for the idea to be the youth's. The more the choice is the youth's, the greater the likelihood he or she will act on it. The following example illustrates this idea:

> A 12-year-old youth refused to do his daily chores and interrupted others doing theirs. The situation started to escalate when youth who were being interrupted became frustrated. A RYCW tried to reason with the 12-year-old to no avail. The same RYCW then said, "Curtis, I'm sure you have a plan because I've seen you think ahead . . . I'm just wondering if you planned to do your chore in 5 minutes or 10 minutes so we could get going to the park and play basketball." Curtis paused briefly before blurting out, "Neither! My plan is do it now!"

Use Distraction

When in a state of crisis, it can seem as if youth are in a trance-like state. They will develop a glazed look, come across as disconnected from others, and act in ways they may not otherwise remember. In such cases distraction can be a way to reorient youth to the current context (i.e., person, place, time, and situation) and shift their attention to other less stress-provoking things. For example, a RYCW might say to a youth who is very angry, "Oh wow, I forgot to wear a belt today!" or "What's your favorite song?" or "I never noticed how blue the walls are in this room. What do you think about the color of the walls?" Methods of distraction may seem silly. The point is to shift the youth's attention. The more a RYCW knows about a particular youth, the more he or she can attempt to distract through things familiar to the youth (e.g., music, television shows, and other interests). RYCWs can sing or hum, tell stories, or change what they are doing physically (e.g., sit on the floor, start doing

138　*In the Moment*

push-ups, etc.). Used effectively, distraction can reduce crisis situations quickly, as shown through the following example:

> A RYCW was working with a youth who started hurling curse words because he thought a situation to be unfair. When the youth was asked what specifically he thought was unfair, he did not respond but instead glared at the RYCW. Another RYCW across the room saw the scenario unfolding and dropped to the floor. The RYCW proceeded to do 10 push-ups before declaring, "I don't think anyone in this room can beat that." In all, three youth took up the challenge, including the one who had been swearing up a storm, who did a total of 38 push-ups.

Use Humor

Humor can reduce the intensity of crisis situations. It can also make things worse if it is perceived as mocking or insincere. Used effectively, humor can serve several purposes in crises. First, it provides a way of engaging youth. Youth who feel well-connected to adults are less likely to remain in a heightened state of tension when in crisis and are more likely to respond to messages that encourage calmness and positive choices. Appropriate humor can also defuse crises by shifting attention and changing emotional states. For example, a youth who laughs will find it difficult to be angry at the same time. Or, with a youth who is threatening self-harm, humor can trigger positive emotions that can lead youth out of negative thinking. It is important that humor not be used to minimize how a youth feels or in a way that is seen as mocking. Here's an example of how to use humor:

> A RYCW was trying to break up an argument between two youth. Given the intensity of the disagreement, the RYCW started to dance. The fact that the RYCW did not know how to dance did not stop him. The two youth who were arguing immediately burst out laughing and began to critique the silliness of the RYCW's gyrations. The RYCW played along, acting as if he had no idea why it was so funny and that he needed to "work on his moves" to prepare for an audition on *America's Got Talent*.

It is a good idea for RYCWs to talk with each other about different strategies of de-escalation. Although some methods will not work with certain youth, and nothing works all the time, the sharing of ideas can get the creative juices flowing. In addition, the bulk of learning takes place both in preparation and reflection.

Working as Part of On-Call Systems

RYCWs often find themselves as part of on-call systems. They may be contacted by youth, caregivers, or program staff who or are in or dealing with crisis situations. In such cases the ideas in the previous section continue to serve as a guide for promoting safety and preventing crises from worsening. In cases in which the severity of a situation cannot be reduced and/or safety cannot be ensured, the result may include outcomes such as discharge of youth from a program, medical or psychiatric hospitalization, involvement of law enforcement, and so on. RYCWs will want to follow the policies and procedures of their organizations in terms of protocols for managing crisis situations.

When RYCWs Contact On-Call Staff

For RYCWs who are considering contacting an on-call supervisor for support with a challenging situation, to determine how to proceed with a crisis, or for the purposes of consultation, the following points can serve as guidance:

1. Before contacting the on-call person, take a deep breath to slow your breathing and clear your mind. Slow things down just a bit so you will be better prepared to communicate clearly with the person on the other end.
2. What is the primary concern for which the on-call person is being contacted? Remember to use action-talk to assist with describing the specifics of the situation. Lack of clarity can lead to frustration with all involved.
3. Try to remain as objective as possible in describing what is happening with the person on-call. Emotions may run high, which can affect how problems are conveyed and in decision making.
4. Consider what you want or need from the person on-call. For example, do you want to bounce your ideas off another staff member? Do you need help with problem solving?
5. Try to avoid getting caught up in the "why" of the situation. There will be time later for exploring theories of causation, but in the midst of a crisis, focus should be on safety and resolving the problem at hand.
6. Let the person on-call know what has been tried unsuccessfully, what might have worked to any degree, and ideas you might have about what to do. Doing so will lead to more productive conversations and minimize time wasted on things that won't really help in the moment.

140   *In the Moment*

7. Before disconnecting from the person on-call, be sure you are clear about what you will do once the call ends.
8. If working with another RYCW or staff person, communicate a plan of action along with who is responsible or doing what and when.

When RYCWs Are On-Call

Being on-call can be an anxiety-provoking experience, yet it does not have to be. One way to reduce any anxiety about being an on-call support is by maintaining self-awareness. When you are on-call, prepare ahead of time by knowing what you will do if contacted for support, to assist with making decisions, or if needed to take a more direct role in resolving crises. There is no reason to rearrange your life if you are on-call—a little preparation is all that is needed. For example, you might let others who you will be with know that you might be contacted and that you may need to step away for a period of time. Or, if out in public, you might identify places you could go to talk privately, if needed. It can also be helpful to let those who are most likely to contact you know if you will be in a place or situation that might take you longer to respond (e.g., meeting with another youth, at a theater, etc.) and what to do if that should happen.

To be as helpful as possible as on-call consultants, RYCWs do the following:

1. Listen, acknowledge, and validate youth, caregivers, or colleagues who call for support. Doing so can help calm situations and increase the likelihood of attaining useful information. Oftentimes acknowledgment of what callers are experiencing can neutralize the anxiety of situations.
2. Collaborate with callers. Utilize their expertise and knowledge. Communicate reassurance.
3. Stay focused by asking callers about their concerns, using action-talk to gain clear descriptions of what is happening that precipitated the call. Avoid getting sidetracked by conversational threads or stories that do not immediately contribute to understanding the problem at hand. Stick to the facts.
4. Focus on safety.
5. Consider what minimally needs to be different to improve the situation.
6. If there is time, find out what has been tried to remedy the situation. Sometimes things that have been helpful in the past have been forgotten in times of crisis. When possible solutions, even partial ones, are identified, if appropriate, encourage those solutions to be imported into the present situation.
7. Explore for options as opposed to "the" answer.
8. Before disconnecting have the person on the other end convey his or her understanding of what to do following the contact.
9. Follow up.

In the Moment 141

The following is an example of how an on-call RYCW might talk with another RYCW to help resolve a crisis:

ON-CALL RYCW: Hello.

RYCW: [Seemingly out of breath] Hi, this is James. I have a situation with a youth here. He is screaming at other kids on the unit, and it's got everyone dialed-up. I think it could get worse.

ON-CALL RYCW: I'm glad you called, James. We're going to work together on this so I need you to take a deep breath, okay?

JAMES: [Breathes deeply] Okay, I'm good.

ON-CALL RYCW: Who else is on shift with you?

JAMES: Carrie is here. She's with the residents—except Paul who is still yelling.

ON-CALL RYCW: Is he threatening to hurt himself or anyone or is he just yelling?

JAMES: He hasn't made threats, he just keep saying "I hate this place" and "I want to get out of here!"

ON-CALL RYCW: Okay. Where is he now?

JAMES: He's in the kitchen.

ON-CALL RYCW: Are others with him in the kitchen or is he by himself?

JAMES: He's by himself.

ON-CALL RYCW: And can you see him from where you are?

JAMES: I can.

ON-CALL RYCW: Have you and Carrie been able to communicate about what to do?

JAMES: There hasn't been time. I told her I would call the on-call.

ON-CALL RYCW: That was a good idea. How have you kept things safe and the situation from escalating further?

JAMES: Well, Carrie got the attention of the eight other youth here and took them into the basement. I told Paul he could yell all he wanted but he needed to stay in the kitchen. That may have been the wrong thing to do. I don't know.

ON-CALL RYCW: You two coordinated things well and what you told Paul, James, was fine. Yelling isn't going to hurt him or anyone else. So it sounds like things are hectic but under control.

JAMES: It didn't seem like that when I called, but, yeah, things are under control. Paul just stopped yelling.

ON-CALL RYCW: You and Carrie are doing a good job. What do you think about talking with Paul? Or do you think it would be better to wait a bit?

JAMES: I think now that he seems calmer I can try to talk to him. Then I can call you back if I need to.

ON-CALL RYCW: Before I let you go, can you tell me a little about how you plan to approach Paul?

JAMES: He likes hockey so I thought I would talk about that.

ON-CALL RYCW: Good idea. And what if he doesn't want to talk?

142   *In the Moment*

JAMES: Then I'll back off and give him some space.

ON-CALL RYCW: Also a good idea. And were you planning on updating Carrie on your plan?

JAMES: Yeah, I'll do that first.

ON-CALL RYCW: Just give me a call back if you need to.

JAMES: Okay, got it. Thanks.

In many cases those consulting with on-call supervisors will be able to resolve concerns with support. It will be a matter of "two heads being better than one." In other instances on-call personnel will be more active in problem solving and in finding solutions. An important reminder for on-call staff is that RYCWs or other staff who are calling have abilities to solve problems. We want to evoke frontline staff strengths in moments of crisis to empower them.

We must also bear in mind that the methods described in this section are reliant on the strengths-based principles outlined in Chapter 2. Whether engaging with youth or other staff, we activate strengths, build relationships, attend to cultural sensitivities, emphasize well-being, and rehabilitate hope by helping those involved in crisis situations exercise their muscles of resilience and refocus their energies on the future. It should be noted that although we do not wish for crises to hone our skills, experience gained is an asset for future situations. As discussed, practice is crucial to skill development. For example, role-plays can assist RYCWs with internalizing methods of preventions, considerations should crisis arise, and possible interventions.

A final point is post-crisis debriefings (PCD). PCDs involve discussion of crisis situations with staff. Usually a lead RYCW, supervisor, or other staff person serves as a mediator, asking some or all of the questions that follow:

1. How was the safety of the youth and others ensured?
2. How did the crisis end?
3. What helped bring the crisis to an end (or prevent it from getting worse)?
4. What did staff do that was helpful? What else?
5. What else, in general, worked in this particular crisis situation?
6. Was there staff consultation during the crisis? If so, what was helpful about the consultation?
7. What, if anything, should to be done differently in regard to safety?
8. What was learned from this incident?
9. What, if anything, should be done differently in the future?
10. What, if anything, might have prevented this particular crisis?
11. What else may be helpful in preventing future crises?

As we have learned, exception seeking is essential to residential settings. When it comes to crises, crises are in fact the exceptions. They are not the norm. We must remember that our programs are 99% crisis free (of the kind of crises that produce serious outcomes). To wit, focusing on what RYCWs do each and every day that works should be part of routine evaluation and program "check-ups." Of course, it is clear to all RYCWs and YFS staff that it only takes one crisis to change a youth's life and/ or to devastate a program. So in the event of a crisis, the best response is timely reflection.

PCDs are mechanisms for reflection, and research makes it clear that a substantial part of learning occurs through reflection. In the case of PCDs, reflection creates an opportunity to identify what worked (to any degree), what did not, and the specific responses of staff. Information attained can then be used to reinforce strengths, determine any areas of concern that need to be addressed, improve on current strategies of prevention, and clarify directions for training staff. The latter point is particularly important given that it is common in YFS following a crisis to provide further training. The problem with this kind of reaction is that more training does not always lead to better outcomes. Crisis debriefings can inform training by revealing areas of strength—those efforts that should be continuously implemented by staff—and areas of growth for individual RYCWs and teams.

7 The Circle of Lives
Future Roads of Possibility

In this final chapter, we will explore two distinct areas, both of which tie together the ideas presented throughout this book. The first relates to how to approach improvement or lack thereof in residential services. A theme throughout this book has been on the benefit of services. To this end, ways of amplifying and anchoring change will also be offered. The second area explored in this chapter is a brief discussion of concerns for RYCWs to heed in continuing careers in YFS.

The Journey of 1,000 Miles: Steps of Any Length

There is a saying, "The journey of 1,000 miles begins with one step." A central premise of a collaborative, strengths-based approach is a focus on the future—one step at a time. In accordance, whether short- or long-term, as youth participate in residential programs and as strategies and interventions are used, we want to determine whether and to what degree there is forward progress. We want to know what is working and what is not. We pay careful attention to what youth communicate verbally and nonverbally through language and interaction. Does a youth talk as if things are better? Unchanged? Worse? What can be inferred from their body language? And we are sure to use action-talk to clarify unclear or vague, nondescriptive terms so we are not assuming incorrectly or misinterpreting situations. In addition to observations and youth descriptions, as mentioned in Chapter 5, the use of formal outcome measurement is highly recommended. We must work toward valid and reliable forms of measuring change for all parties involved (i.e., clients, funders, donors, etc.) to fully appreciate the effectiveness of residential services. The use of formal outcome measurement in YFS is described elsewhere (see Bertolino, 2014).

Also discussed in Chapter 5 were two categories of responses of youth to intervention strategies. These responses include *no improvement or deterioration* and *improvement*. In the next section, we will consider options for RYCWs in responding to youth who are either not improving or getting worse. Following this we will learn about possibilities for building on improvement, including how to share positive change with others.

Sooner Rather Than Later: We're Not Getting Anywhere or Even *Worse*

Routine and ongoing monitoring of outcome—how youth are faring in services—should be part of any residential program. This is particularly important as research indicates that by and large mental health professionals do poorly when it comes to identifying valid and reliable change. Whereas achievement of goals or breaking rules are obvious behavioral markers, outcome is related to individual, interpersonal, and social roles functioning. Further, lack of improvement early in services without a change in response by service providers is a consistent predictor of both dropout and negative outcome. In short, we need to know sooner rather than later how youth are responding to our residential programs.

There are two ways that youth are said to not be progressing in services. The first is *no improvement*, which means that a youth has expressed a continuation of roughly the same degree of distress (within a predefined range) and/or well-being based on formal instrumentation, verbal statements by youth, or staff observation. With the latter youth will usually provide statements such as, "Nothing's different" or "It still sucks here." Again, formal instrumentation is considered more reliable but does not replace the observation skills of RYCWs.

A second way is *deterioration*, which suggests that a youth has expressed an increase the degree of distress (within a predefined range) and/or well-being based on formal instrumentation, verbal statements by youth, or staff observation. When youth are deteriorating they will typically verbalize their distress through statements such as, "Things keep getting worse" or "Every day I feel like the walls are closing in. Why should I try?" These sorts of statements are not out of the ordinary. Some will reflect the ups and downs of youth. However, because drops can indicate many things, it is important that RYCWs explore the meaning of both outcome scores and youth comments. It is especially important to respond to deterioration as it is highly correlated with frustration and loss of hope, which are precursors for dropout (Garcia & Weisz, 2002) and negative outcome (Warren et al., 2010), two of the most significant threats to YFS as a whole.

When there has been no change or there is evidence of deterioration, RYCWs respond quickly, yet carefully. Because lack of progress is correlated with negative outcome, we focus on two things. First, is to check the alliance—the quality of the relationships youth have with staff. Are youth engaged with staff? We ask youth questions such as these:

- How do you know staff are listening and understanding you when you talk with them?
- What should staff do more or less of when talking with you?

146   *The Circle of Lives*

- What would be most helpful for staff to know about how you prefer to relate?
- Who on staff here do you feel is easiest for you to talk to?
- What does that person do to help you feel better listened to and understood?
- What do you find most helpful about how [staff] talks with you?
- What difference does that make for you?
- What other staff would you would be willing to give a chance to sit down and talk with you?

Knowing what youth value in relationships helps create more of a safe hiding environment from which positive change can emanate. Sometimes small adjustments to the alliance will make a difference to increase the fit of future interventions. The following questions can also help with exploring ruptures in relationships between RYCWs and youth and supportive others:

- Discuss the here-and-now relationship with the youth and supportive others involved.
- Ask for further feedback.
- Create space and allow the youth or supportive others to assert any negative feelings.
- Engage in conversations about the youth or supportive other's expectations and preferences.
- Discuss the match between the RYCW's style and the youth or supportive others' preferred ways of relating.
- Spend more time learning about the youth or supportive others' experience in services.
- Readdress the agreement established about goals and tasks to accomplish those goals.
- Accept responsibility as a service provider for your part in alliance ruptures.
- Normalize the youth or supportive other's responses by stating that talking about concerns, facing challenges, taking action, and/or therapy in general can be difficult.
- Provide rationale for techniques and methods.
- Attend closely to subtle clues (e.g., nonverbal behaviors, patterns such as one-word answers) that may indicate a problem with the alliance.
- Offer more positive feedback and encouragement (except when the youth communicates either verbally or nonverbally that this is not a good match; Safran, Muran, Samstang, & Stevens, 2002).

A second thing for RYCWs to focus on when there is no change or even deterioration is how youth and supportive others have kept things from getting worse. In Chapter 5, a series of coping sequence questions was offered. These questions ask: What's kept things from getting worse?

The Circle of Lives   147

Exceptions can provide opportunities to stop downward slides and shift momentum in a more positive direction.

A further consideration with youth who seem to be struggling is to talk more openly with youth about possible points of impasse. In most cases youth are very aware that things are not improving, and yet it is not their job to bring up problems or identify where services are breaking down. We must take initiative to open up conversations to move things forward. Next are some areas for RYCWs to consider with this:

- Assess the youth's state of readiness to take action to change something about his or her situation.
- Focus more on the youth's view of the problem or situation.
- Ask open-ended questions that will allow the youth to notice one or more aspects that have been downplayed or have gone unnoticed (take care not to imply that the youth's perspective is "wrong"; instead, try only to introduce other ways of viewing that may offer new possibilities or will encourage the youth to talk about the problem or situation differently).
- Help the youth weigh the possible positive and negative effects of his or her behavior.
- Help the youth weigh the possible benefits and drawbacks of change.
- Offer straightforward feedback without imposing it (for example, "From where I am standing, I'm concerned about what might happen if this continues. Of course, that is for you to decide, but I believe it's my responsibility to speak about it."). (Note: Always provide more directive feedback and make necessary safeguards if there is risk of harm to self or others.)
- Demonstrate genuine confidence that the youth has the strength to face his or her challenges.
- Avoid a "solution-forced" situation when the youth's preference is to talk more about problems and his or her ambivalence.
- Acknowledge further—ensure that the youth feels heard and understood and verifies this either verbally or nonverbally (ask questions or use an alliance measure as needed).
- Reorient to the youth's concerns to ensure that you and the youth are focusing on the same issue.
- Discuss with persons who have the authority to begin or end services whether the level of services is a good fit.

When you are struggling in residential services, the easy thing to do would be to pin the lack of progress on them—to refer to you as motivated, resistant, noncompliant, and a host of other negative descriptors. Most people in a residential program will feel deflated, discouraged, and hopeless at some point. Residential programs are not and will not substitute for a loving, supportive family environment. But, and this is crucial, residential

148 *The Circle of Lives*

programs are places where youth can experience love, compassion, support, and opportunity. So we must do our absolute best, every day, to look at ourselves when things are not going well. When progress stalls we reorient to our personal philosophies. It is our best resource in hard times. Perspective is expressed through character, which, in turn, reveals itself in adversity. And youth need our support most in the midst of adversity.

The Benefits Seen: Everyone Wins

When youth benefit and improve in residential programs, everyone wins. Youth benefit. Relationships benefit. Communities, society, and the world at large benefit. How? Youth are more likely to achieve their dreams, to live the lives they want. They will come in contact with others and support those persons and enrich their lives. Cycles of violence will end. Communities and societies will be stronger because the youth from our programs will be making contributions. This is how residential programs can play a big role in the future. Far-fetched? Absolutely not. Who will raise youth who are otherwise homeless, cast away, and unsupported? We will.

To help youth achieve their futures, we have become better at identifying and amplifying improvement and positive change. By *improvement* we mean that a youth has expressed a decrease in the degree of distress (within a predefined range) and/or improvement in well-being based on formal instrumentation, verbal statements by youth, or staff observation. Monitoring progress from the outset of services means we are not only able to distinguish youth who are reporting no improvement or even deterioration but those who are rating their lives and situations as improved. RYCWs want to explore any form of positive change as it may serve as a building block to more significant, sweeping changes. In contrast, change that is considered reliable and valid will have to be measured formally, which is another reason for a residential program to commit to standardized outcome measurement.

Exceptions again provide a doorway into the lives of youth. We can begin to understand improvement by first considering indicators of change in general. Here are some questions to help with this:

- What have you noticed that has changed with your concern/problem/ self/situation?
- What specifically seems to be going better?
- Who first noticed that things had changed?
- Who else noticed the change?
- When did you first notice that things had changed?
- What did you notice happening?

With information from one or more of these questions, we can focus on *how* the change occurred and *what* factors appeared to contribute to it.

The Circle of Lives 149

We do this by asking questions that draw on specific actions of youth. We also emphasize any differences that the change has made in relation to goals. The questions that follow are used to amplify change:

- How did the change happen?
- What do you think might have influenced that positive change? [e.g., family, other support, culture]
- What worked for you?
- What specifically did you do?
- How did you get yourself to do that?
- How was what you did different than before?
- Where did you get the idea to do things that way?
- What role, if any, did others play in helping move things forward?
- How specifically did others support and/or help you?

Should youth struggle with questions about improvement, it may be that the questions asked are too global or general. In such cases, looking for smaller changes may prove more fruitful. To do this, YCWs might say, "How did you get that change to happen just a little?" or "What did you do a little differently than in past situations?" YCWs need only identify granules or ripples of change, which can then be developed into bigger ones.

Answers to exception-oriented questions can help us better understand how youth use their strengths and resources to manage problems. Doing so is an integral part of change processes because it often helps youth and others around them recognize abilities that have gone unnoticed or underutilized. Action-talk again plays a role in following up on improvement since youth will often give vague answers when asked how change occurred. They will say, "I don't know, I just did it" or "Things just got better." As we take care to clarify, as best as we can, what change and how that change occurred, we are also accepting of the answer "I don't know." Truly, sometimes you do not know. Still, accepting "I don't know" does not mean giving up on learning more about positive change. Instead we change directions.

Presuppose Clarity About Change

One way of changing directions is to use what is known in hypnosis as a posthypnotic suggestion. We say to youth, "Maybe things will become a bit clearer shortly" or "Perhaps in a few days or a week you'll have a better idea of how things began to get better for you." The idea is to orient the attention of youth toward the future by presupposing that they will come to new understandings. This shifts focus to improvement and change as opposed to how youth might return to the full-blown problem pattern.

150   *The Circle of Lives*

Speculate About Change

A second way RYCWs can help identify how improvement came about is through *speculation*. Speculation involves RYCWs combining conjecture or curiosity with guesswork about how change might have come about (Bertolino, 2003). For example, a RYCW might have a youth speculate or guess by asking, "If you had to guess, and there were no wrong answers, what would you say made a difference for you?" or "If [e.g., a close friend, mother, teacher] were here, what would he/she say has contributed to things changing?" If these sorts of questions do not reveal anything, RYCWs can do their own speculating, "What do you think about the idea that you might have had a role in your situation improving?" This inquiry can then be followed up with questions to assist with developing speculation:

- I'm wondering if perhaps part of the reason things are going better for you is that you are becoming [e.g., more in tune with what you want, more responsible, more mature, wiser, growing up]. Perhaps you are becoming the type of person you want to be and learning new ways of managing your life. What do you think about this idea?
- Is it possible that the changes you've made are indications that [you're thinking more about how your actions affect others or are wanting others to know the "real" you]?
- Is it possible that the change you've experienced might be related to you wanting life be different in some way?
- What do you think about the idea that the change you've experienced might be related to your [e.g., wanting to lead a different life, being ready for the next stage of your life]?
- What do you think about the idea that the change you've experienced might be an indication that you're taking back control of your life?
- How might the change you've experienced be a sign of a new, preferred direction for you?

When using speculation we leave it up to youth to either accept or reject what has been said. When RYCWs' speculations involve the attribution of positive qualities and actions, they are less likely to be rejected. It would be unlikely for a youth will say, "No, I'm becoming less thoughtful of others" or "No, I'm actually getting more and more immature." Even if speculations are off target, because they highlight competencies, youth will at least reflect on them. It can be very empowering for youth to know that someone sees them in a new, different, and evolving light. And by RYCWs or others offering explanations, it is hopeful that youth will develop their own. The following case example illustrates the effects of speculation:

The Circle of Lives 151

> Trey, a 14-year-old, was mandated to therapy by the family court. He and a friend had stolen his friend's mother's ATM card and withdrawn more than $2,000. Trey had also been failing his classes at school. Over the course of 7 months, Trey made amends and paid restitution for the theft and raised his grades in school. He did this by turning in his homework and doing extra credit. To his mother's surprise, he also began helping out at home by mowing the lawn and cleaning. When asked what he thought led him to make so many changes, Trey appeared somewhat confused and answered, "I'm not sure. I guess I just did it." I followed this by speculating about some possibilities by saying, "I wonder if it's because you are becoming more mature and responsible. Maybe you're also thinking more about others, like your mom." His eyes glistening, Trent leaned forward and said, "Yeah, I think that's part of it. I also think I'm just seeing that things need to be done and no one can do them but me. I've done it and I'm proud."

Attribute

When youth have articulated thoughts about how change took place, they will often attribute change to external factors—things outside of themselves and their control. Youth will adhere to the idea that improvement is the result of medication, residential staff or other helpers, or services, for example. And the more that youth attribute change to external factors, the more internal locus of control decreases and the more likely the change will endure or "stick." This is in part because personal accountability dissipates once external factors have been removed or diminish as causal agents of change.

RYCWs can counter the influence of external attribution by attributing the majority of positive change to youth. Essentially, RYCWs essentially "blame" youth for changing for the better (Bertolino, 2014). To do this RYCWs ask questions to assist in assigning change:

- How is that you have been able face so many challenges and not lose sight of _____?
- Who are you such that you've been able to _____?
- What does the fact that you've been able to face up to _____ say about you?
- What kind of person are you that you've been able to overcome _____?
- Where did you get the wherewithal to _____?

These questions draw focus to the contributions of youth but do not imply that external factors are irrelevant. Rather, external factors

152 *The Circle of Lives*

influence whereas youth are engineers of change. RYCWs take care to acknowledge the contributions of external influences while simultaneously attributing change to the overall actions of youth. Here are some questions to assist with this process:

- You said that [i.e., parent, caregiver, other form of support, etc.] has always been there for you. How has his/her involvement helped you with what you've been going through? How did you use his/her support as a stepping stone to take steps toward your future?
- You mentioned that [i.e., parent, caregiver, other form of support, etc.] was supportive of you in overcoming the problem that brought you to see us. How did his/her support help you take action toward the future you've envisioned for yourself?
- You mentioned that you feel/think that [e.g., medication, services] is helping. How are you working with the [e.g., medication, services] to better your life?
- In your mind, what does [e.g., medication, services] allow you to do that you might not have otherwise done?
- What percentage of the change you've experienced is a result of [e.g., medication, services], and what percentage do you think is the result of your own doing? Tell me about the changes you've made on your own.
- As a result of feeling better from [e.g., medication, services], what are you now able to do? What specifically do you do now that is in the direction of goals you have for yourself?

All RYCWs encounter youth who struggle to identify what has brought about or contributed to positive change. Youth often respond to questions with "I don't know" or by shrugging their shoulders. These kinds of "empty" replies do not mean that youth are withholding information or are resistant; they may not have given much thought to it, really do not know, or perhaps are not interested. Rather than pushing youth to come up with answers, RYCWs consider the aforementioned responses of youth only as communication, and such communication calls for RYCWs to *do something different* (Bertolino, 2014).

Speculation and attribution are just two possibilities for drawing attention to the contributions you have made to change their lives. They also support evolving new stories of growth, resiliency, and hope that run counter to the problem-saturated ones. New stories serve as an "anchor" for change, meaning that youth are better able to connect with their internal experiences, including feelings and sensory perceptions (Bertolino, 1999). By moving to an experiential level, the change may be more profound. To further assist youth in connecting with internal experiences, RYCWs ask questions such as these:

- When you were able to [action], what did that feel like?
- How did you experience that change inside?

The Circle of Lives   153

- How was that feeling similar or different than before?
- What does it feel like to know that others may also benefit from the changes you've made?

Sharing Credit for Change

When working with families, other caregivers, or those in support of youth in residential settings, it can be important to share credit for positive change. It is particularly important when youth will be transitioning to settings such as home. We want to impart the idea that although youth are the ones who made the changes, no one is successful without the support of others. And future success will involve the ongoing support of many persons.

Unlike attribution, sharing the credit involves focusing on relationships and acknowledging each person's contribution to improving overall situations. Sharing the credit serves several purposes. First, as you have learned, the quality of the client's (in this case youth and families) participation in services is an important factor in outcome. When involved persons are left out of therapeutic processes, they can appear as noncompliant, resistant, and unmotivated. By recognizing the contributions of supportive others, RYCWs are extending change to those who may be more peripherally involved but are nonetheless important to the stability of the youth's relationships and/or social networks (Bertolino, 2014).

Second, sharing the credit can serve as a countermeasure in situations where positive change has occurred but is being negated in some way. This is most often evidenced by caregiver statements such as, "It will never last," "He's done that before," or "You haven't seen the real [youth's name] yet." These comments sometimes originate from caregivers or supportive others who do not feel as if they have made a valued or positive contribution to the improvement of the youth. Consider what a caregiver, such as a parent, might experience when change happens quickly in services. A parent gives her all to raise her daughter. Because her daughter gets into trouble, the parent begins to feel her efforts were to no avail. So she seeks services for her daughter, who begins to turn things around. And it works. The daughter improves. But the result has also raised feelings of self-blame on the part of the mother ("I'm a bad parent," "I clearly did a bad job") or inadequacy ("I obviously don't know what I'm doing," "Anyone could do a better job than me").

Caregiver experiences of invalidation and feelings of failure can undermine services. The irony is that although family members are sometimes considered the cause of problems, they do not always get credit for their contributions when things go better. By identifying the contributions of everyone who may be involved, RYCWs counter negative statements that can minimize change and prove invalidating. There are several

154   *The Circle of Lives*

possibilities for sharing the credit for change. One way is to give others involved with services credit by saying words such as these:

- I wonder how you were able to instill the value of [specific value] in [youth's name].
- Like you, [youth's name] seems to hold the value of [specific value]. I can't help thinking that he/she learned it from you.
- It seems to me that [youth's name] has learned the value of [specific value] from you.

A second possibility is to evoke from those involved something that they feel contributed to the change process:

- How do you think your [relationship, parenting, etc.] has contributed to [youth's name]'s ability to [action]?
- In what ways do you think you have been able to help [youth's name] stand up to adversity?
- In what ways do you think you were of assistance in helping [youth's name] stand up to [concern/problem] and get back on track?

A third way is to ask the youth what contributions others have made to his or her life and then to share the answers with others who are involved:

- What did you learn from [name] about how to overcome [concern/problem]?
- Who taught you the value of [specific value]?
- From whom did you learn about [action, thing]?

The preceding questions do not create conflict in attributing change to the qualities and actions of individuals but offer "both/and" as opposed to "either/or." RYCWs both attribute the major portion of significant change to individuals and share the credit with those who have provided care and support. Doing so can neutralize each person's feelings that their efforts have been acknowledged but are valued negatively. As a result of sharing the credit for change, it is not uncommon for youth and others who are involved to experience a new sense of togetherness or spirit of family (Bertolino, 2014).

Beyond the Immediate: Developing the New Story

When positive change occurs and there is some identifiable benefit to youth and supportive others, there are opportunities to build further momentum toward the future. And we want to build momentum so that youth are better able to weather challenges that may arise as they continue toward the futures they want for themselves. One of the ways we can do with this youth in residential settings is by collecting good news and then finding avenues to share it. In the sections that follow, we explore possibilities for broadening the new stories of hope youth are experiencing, helping them rewrite their life stories (Bertolino, 1999).

Good news about youth (e.g., academic achievement, sports successes, community contributions, etc.) appears in the news or social media every day. This kind of attention can help amplify and spread new, valued stories about youth. We believe this sharing with larger contexts can strengthen these valued stories. Freeman, Epston, and Lobovits (1997) remarked, "The process of gathering information to share with others invites further 'performance of meaning,' thereby strengthening the narrative" (p. 125). This sharing of good news is especially important given that much of what is communicated about youth is negative.

With youth in residential programs, we want to amplify positive change, overcoming adversity, reaching graduation, or some success through those mediums that are most meaningful. There are very practical ways of sharing these accomplishments. What follows is a way to do this.

Collecting Evidence

Take a moment to ask yourself, "When I was growing up, did my parents/caregivers keep track of my accomplishments in some way?" If you can answer this question in the affirmative, consider how those who raised you did this. Did they use scrapbooks, or file your papers someplace accessible, or perhaps post things on the refrigerator or place your artwork on the walls? Many happy memories are attached to meaning of overcoming obstacles, getting good grades, graduating, and so on.

RYCWs can encourage and participate in the process of accentuating accomplishment by helping youth collect evidence of success. We can, for example, help youth start scrapbooks or journals or create posters or collage signifying change over a designated length of time or punctuating specific event. The collection of evidence can be done on a one-time basis or in an ongoing way. They then form "collections of competence" that can be shared with other youth in a program, staff, or whomever youth choose (Bertolino, 1999). Here's a way of talking with youth about getting started collecting evidence and tracking change:

> Down the road, others may be curious as to how you managed to get the upper hand with _____. Sometimes scrapbooks, diaries, videos, and similar things are used to keep track of accomplishments. I'm wondering how we can start to keep track of your movement forward. What do you think about this? What ideas do you have that might work for you?

156 *The Circle of Lives*

The idea of collecting evidence of change is illustrated through the following example:

> Twelve-year-old Owen was meek and shy. He struggled to get a word in edgewise with his peers. And Owen often felt like the other youth in the program were making fun of him—seeing him as inept and unskilled. When I met with Owen he said he wasn't good at anything. So I suggested that we do an experiment to test out the view he had of himself. The experiment involved both of us tracking what Owen did over the course of 2 weeks, then reviewing the results together. I gave Owen a scrapbook and suggested that he keep track of any "evidence" of success and put it in the scrapbook. Evidence could be anything that occurred since he had entered the program 6 months earlier up until the 2-week mark we had set.
>
> At the end of the first week, Owen and I met. Owen was beaming with excitement. He had a grin from ear to ear. With an air of confidence, Owen opened his scrapbook and exclaimed, "Look!" I poured over a series of artifacts Owen had collected in the matter of just a few days. He had assignments from school with high grades, letters from other RYCWs, and approved level promotions. I confirmed to Owen that he had gathered amazing evidence and all in just 1 week's time! Owen took great pride in his accomplishments and realized ability that had gone unnoticed, which helped to change the story he had about himself.

Another possibility is to use "letters of evidence" that punctuate specific instances of positive change and success (see Table 7.1). These letters are completed by RYCWs, other staff, teachers, or others who have observed youth succeeding in some way. For example, a teacher might note that a youth had been on time to class for a week straight or had completed his or her class assignments. Letters of evidence as well as other forms of competence can be then be compiled into an "evidence log" (see Table 7.2; Bertolino, 1999). RYCWs can then review these evidence logs. Collected evidence can be kept as a reminder of accomplishment or could be used during "home visits" to show progress to caregivers. This again helps youth and others in support of youth focus on what's right. A further benefit is that youth can keep their collections of evidence and revisit them in the future.

Amplifying: Maintaining Forward Momentum

As evidence of positive change begins to emerge, we keep in mind that a change in one area can lead to one or more changes in another. RYCWs continue to scan for ways in which positive change may be creating a "ripple effect." Like a snowball traveling downhill, expanding as it gains

The Circle of Lives 157

Table 7.1 Letter of Evidence

Letter of Evidence
Name of Youth: _____
Week of: _____
Type of Evidence:
_____
_____
_____
_____
_____
_____
_____
_____
_____
_____
Evidence Reported by: _____
Signature of Reporter: _____
Date: _____

speed and momentum, or a domino starting a chain reaction of knocking over others, RYCWs search for other changes in the lives of youth. Questions to assist with the ripples of change include these:

- What else have you noticed that has changed?
- What else is different?
- How has/have that/those difference(s) been helpful to you?
- What difference has the change made with [school/home life/friends/work, etc.]?
- Who else has noticed these other changes?
- Who else has benefited from these changes?
- What difference has that made for him/her/them?

158   *The Circle of Lives*

Table 7.2 Weekly Evidence Log

Weekly Evidence Log
Name of Youth: _____
Week of: _____
☺ 1.
☺ 2.
☺ 3.
☺ 4.
☺ 5.
Signature: _____
Date: _____

As always, action-talk is used to clarify vague responses and to better understand "what" is different and "how" those changes came about. While specific goals are identified from the outset of services, it is not uncommon to learn that secondary concerns or areas are affected and changed in some way. Secondary changes suggest that although identified goals are the main focus, RYCWs remain on the lookout for ways to promote change in general. Doing so can indirectly lead to gains in meeting established goals. It is therefore crucial to ask youth about positive changes or benefits that may have occurred elsewhere in their lives and how those might relate to the concerns that led to services.

As an aside, RYCWs can use *linking*, a means of joining two things that have not been joined together previously (O'Hanlon, 1987). One of the benefits of linking is that it orients youth to other changes that may be occurring concurrently but perhaps without notice. There are two ways to link. The first involves using words including "as," "while," and "when." For example, a RYCW might say, "As you continue your sobriety, you can notice how that increases your enjoyment of other things" or "While you are appreciating your improved school performance, you may also notice the effect it has on your relationship with your friends."

A second way to use linking is by using phrases such as "the more this, the more that"; "the less this, the less that"; "the more this, the less that";

The Circle of Lives   159

or "the less this, the more that." RYCW might say, for example, "The more comfortable you become with sadness, the more accepting you may be of your other feelings" or "The less anxiety you experience, the more you can appreciate the gains you have made." The idea is to help youth notice that change in one area of their lives can trigger change in others.

Understanding the Meaning and Relevance of Change

Residential programs are unique in that youth accomplish goals and yet progress may not be marked with the changes they desire. For example, a youth may achieve many goals and still remain in a program, with few or no future options until they reach a certain age. This also means that service or treatment plans will need to be modified as goals are met. One of the conundrums that residential staff report is that youth will sometimes make great progress only to quickly regress. One of the reasons for this is youth see no incentive for improving beyond a certain point. For example, if a youth gains three levels and more privileges but realizes she will not be returning home, which is what she wants, what is her incentive? Part of becoming an effective RYCW means understanding how to work with youth on things that matter most to them. This is why a vision of the future is so very important. It is also why we have to explore the relevance and meaning of change for both youth and those who have to make decisions (legal guardians) about whether youth will remain in programs, be moved elsewhere, and so on.

The task of the RYCW is to engage youth and others involved in conversations to understand: How does the change that has occurred relate to the goals and outcome defined at the start of services? Further questions include these: Have the concerns or problems been resolved to a degree that a change in situation can occur? What else needs to happen for services to be considered successful/for goals to be met? To understand how change is situated in relationship to goals, the following questions can be helpful to ask of youth:

- What difference has the change made in your life?
- How are you benefiting from the change you've experienced?
- What will be different in the future as these changes continue to occur?
- In the future, what other changes do you think might occur that might not have otherwise come about?
- Who else might benefit from these changes? How?
- In the future, what will indicate to you that these changes are continuing to happen?
- How does the change that's happened relate to the goals that we set?
- What difference has this change made in relation to your goals for treatment?
- To what degree have things improved?

160 *The Circle of Lives*

- Has the problem that brought you here been resolved?
- What else needs to happen to cause this problem to fade from your life?
- What else, if anything, needs to happen so that you'll feel/think that the problem you came here for is manageable?
- What else, if anything, needs to happen so that you'll be convinced that the problem no longer exists?
- Last time, you indicated that if you were able to _____, you would know that things were better. Now that you have achieved this, how do you see things?
- At the start of our work together, you told me that things were at a 3 on a scale of 1 to 10. You also mentioned that you would know that our work together had been successful when _____. That would represent an 8. Now that those things have happened, does that indicate to you that things are at an 8? What else, if anything, needs to happen for you to feel that you have met your goals?

Again the use of reliable and valid methods of measurement raises the bar of accountability in residential programs. In this book the benefits of monitoring both goals and outcomes has been discussed. And yet, because not all residential programs will track both, let's consider evaluating progress exclusively on the basis of one or the other. Let's start with goals.

A primary concern with goals is that they can be met without necessarily having improved outcome. For example, a youth may report that she is meeting goals such as getting school work in on time and getting better grades. However, if the same youth does not report improvement on an outcome measure, further exploration is necessary. This is because the youth may reach concrete goals yet remain depressed or anxious or continue to have trouble in relationships with peers and so on. If goals have been met but are inconsistent with outcome scores, a RYCW might approach the youth by stating, "You've accomplished the goals you set out to achieve and yet you've expressed some [summarize what has been indicated in the outcome measure] in the instrument you completed today. Please tell me about that" (Bertolino, 2014).

Outcomes can also improve without goals being met. Because real-time data can provide snapshots of recent times, RYCWs are reminded that single scores can indicate one-time fluctuations. Large changes in scores are likely to reflect situational changes (e.g., positive events, crises) that may not give an accurate depiction of youth's lives as a whole. RYCWs serve youth best by comparing and contrasting scores over an extended period of time. Improvement, deterioration, or flattening of scores (i.e., very small changes over a span of multiple interactions) is likely to provide a more reliable picture.

Because goals and outcomes can both produce anomalies, using multiple sources of data while sticking to the 80/20 rule (i.e., focus on

The Circle of Lives 161

information that is most meaningful and essential to decision making) is a best practice. In residential settings the duo of goals and outcomes provides a consistent way of evaluating improvement. At the same time, research makes it clear that if a choice has to be made in terms of what kind of data best indicates improvement, an outcomes focus is considerably more reliable (Bertolino, 2014).

Preparing for What's Next

Growth involves age-appropriate independence. For some youth, the path to independence will differ due to circumstances such as being in the custody of the state or moving from program to program throughout childhood and adolescence. For other youth (and their families), chronic situations and perpetuating cycles will translate to services over a lifespan. No matter the situation, RYCWs maintain an unwavering commitment to preparing youth for greater self-sufficiency. To this end, the principles of Positive Youth Development described in Chapter 5 provide a basis for preparing youth for what comes next. PYD involves promoting and fostering characteristics of youth such as rewarding bonds with supportive others, self-determination, positive identity, a future focus, and prosocial norms that reflect clear, healthy, responsible beliefs and behavior. The addition of PYD to goals and outcomes forms an excellent trio of markers for evaluating overall improvement for residential programs (Bertolino, 2014).

The type of transition, whether it's to home, to a foster home, from one program to another, or to setting with more independence, will influence how transition occurs. Although programs will have specific ways of preparing youth for transitions, transition planning is important (Casey et al., 2010). In addition, there are some general areas of focus. We start first with three ways of taking change into the future, including how to cope with adversity, which is a part of life and something that will linger close by for many youth.

Taking Change Forward

A first way to prepare youth for transition is by making sure their successes are clear to them, not just to residential staff. We can do this by using questions aimed at further amplifying change:

- What specifically have you learned while here that will help you no matter where you go?
- How is what you've accomplished in this program going to help you [at home, the next setting, etc.]?
- In what ways do you feel you are different from how you were when you first came here? How can that help you in the future?

162   *The Circle of Lives*

We can also help youth foresee potential hurdles and cope with those challenges effectively. Here are a few questions to help with that process:

- What might come up over the next short while that might present a challenge to you staying on track?
- Is there anything that might happen in the near future that might pose a threat to the changes you've made?
- What's one thing that can bring a slippage under control or to an end?
- Since you've learned new ways of doing things, how will you handle things differently in the future when you encounter something unexpectedly or that challenges you?

A third way of taking change forward is to suggest ongoing focus on the future:

- What will you do in the future, after you leave here, to keep things moving in a direction that is right for you?
- How will you keep yourself pointed in a direction that is best for you?
- How can others help and support you to stay on track?

It is not possible or necessary to cover every situation that could derail a youth. Our aim is to remind youth to use what they have learned more deliberately in the future. In the same vein is a focus on future change in general. Effective programs prepare youth for coping with life beyond the concerns that led to services. By asking questions that orient youth toward future change and progress, they often become more resilient to everyday problems. It is as if their psychological and relational immune systems are less likely to be compromised because they are focusing on health, well-being, and the future (Bertolino, 2014).

Celebrating Transitions and New Life Stories

As youth move on to new life circumstances, we can punctuate changes in an assortment of ways. One way is to have youth explore *who they are* as a result of the new stories that now define their lives. New stories represent new possibilities. In particular they engender the hope that was absent in previous problem-saturated stories. To help youth further develop their new life scripts, RYCWs can ask the following questions:

- What does your decision to stand up to _____ tell you about yourself?
- Now that you've taken your life back from _____, what does that say about the kind of person you are?
- How would you describe yourself now as opposed to when you began services?

The Circle of Lives 163

- What's it like to hear you describe yourself as _____?
- What effect does knowing that you've put _____ to rest have on your view of yourself?
- Can you speculate about how this view of yourself as _____ is changing how you're relating to me right now?
- What do you think _____ would say/think about you since you have come to think of yourself as able to stand up for yourself?
- How do you think my view of you has changed since hearing you describe yourself as _____?
- How do you think _____ will respond to you differently now that they know that you see yourself as a person who is capable of getting the upper hand with _____?

Inviting the perspectives of supportive others is another way to help new stories to take "root." This can be done by asking the following questions:

- What do you think [youth's name]'s decision to stand up to _____ tells you about him/her that you wouldn't have otherwise known?
- What effect might [youth's name]'s decision to regain his/her life back from _____ have on your relationship with him/her?
- How do you think [youth's name]'s new sense of self as being [e.g., capable, independent, responsible] might affect your relationship with him/her?
- What other changes do you foresee as [youth's name] continues on this new path?

If youth have created scrapbooks, journals, or other ways of documenting their changes, they are encouraged to review those successes as time passes. They may also choose to share those changes with others, who may benefit from hearing their stories. What benefits one can benefit others. Whether verbalized, documented, or both, new life stories can also be shared in larger contexts; this can benefit both youth and others who may be experiencing similar difficulties. Examples might involve public speaking, volunteering, writing for a story for a newspaper, and so on. Youth and their families do not have to be on television or write lengthy biographies for their stories to touch others. To pursue this idea, RYCWs can ask these questions:

- Who else needs to know about the changes that you've made?
- What difference do you think it would make in others' attitudes toward you if they had this news?
- Who else could benefit from these changes? How so?
- Would it be better to go along with others' old views about you or to update them on these new developments?

164   *The Circle of Lives*

- What ideas do you have about letting others know about the changes that you've made?
- What might be a first step toward making this happen?

Youth may also become consultants to others. RYCWs can encourage this idea by saying, "Periodically I meet with others who are experiencing the same or a similar problem to the one you've faced. From what you now know, what advice might I give them about facing their concerns?" Or, "What suggestions would you have for RYCWs or mental health professionals who in the future might work with youth who have experienced the same or similar problems?" Despite the benefits of sharing change with others, we remain aware that change can be deeply personal. Some youth may prefer to keep their experiences to themselves.

What is important is for staff to help youth depart on a positive note. Sometimes other youth in a program can be invited to share something meaningful and say good-bye or perhaps write a note of support. Another possibility is to share with all others in the program the successes of a youth. Some programs will use discharge or transition rituals as well. These are events that assist with closure while celebrating the strengths and accomplishments of youth. Transition rituals can also be used with youth who are leaving on less than positive terms. In these cases, rituals are used to send the youth forward with something positive to build on.

Your Last Words: The Message

What message do you want to have youth take with them as they transition out of your program? It is sad but true that we may never see the youth with whom we work again. Leaving youth a message of hope is a valuable gesture. Because opportunities to impart a message of hope as they leave can easily be missed, please think about how you can seize the moment and leave youth with a meaningful word or two.

Thank You for Being You

A few years ago, I was in Las Vegas to speak at a conference. I was having dinner and talking about the day with my wife, Misha, who had arrived on a later flight. She recounted a conversation she had with a gentleman during her flight. After sharing with her that he was in the financial business in Los Angeles, the man asked Misha what she did for a living. She told him she was a Montessori preschool teacher. The man paused and said, "Thank you." I don't know how often people thank you for what you do every day. So I say thank you for your dedication and commitment to youth, each other, and our communities.

It is my hope that you will periodically take time to reflect on your experience as a RYCW. As we know, the average "life" of a RYCW is less than 2 years. Most will move on to other roles and perhaps out of the field altogether. I hope you have found some granules in the form of ideas and strategies that you will use for yourself, not just in your work. To this end, self-care will only be a phrase if not practiced every day. Keep front and center those things that revitalize and invigorate you. Know what inspires and moves you. And most of all, know just how important you are to the present and future youth. We need you.

References

American Psychiatric Association (APA). (2013). *The diagnostic and statistical manual of mental disorders* (5th ed.). Washington, DC: American Psychiatric Publishing.

Anderson, T., Ogles, B. M., Patterson, C. L., Lambert, M. J., & Vermeersch, D. A. (2009). Therapist effects: Facilitative interpersonal skills as a predictor of therapist effects. *Journal of Clinical Psychology, 65*(7), 755–768.

Appelstein, C. D. (1998). *No such thing as a bad kid: Understanding and responding to the challenging behavior of troubled children and youth.* Weston, MA: The Gifford School.

Bachelor, A., & Horvath, A. (1999). The therapeutic relationship. In S. D. Miller (Ed.), *The heart and soul of change: What works in therapy* (pp. 133–178). Washington, DC: American Psychological Association.

Baldwin, S. A., Wampold, B. E., & Imel, Z. E. (2007). Untangling the alliance-outcome correlation: Exploring the relative importance of therapist and patient variability in the alliance. *Journal of Consulting and Clinical Psychology, 75*(6), 842–852.

Barford, S. W., & Whelton, W. J. (2010). Understanding burnout in child and youth care workers. *Child Youth Care Forum, 39,* 271–287.

Bertolino, B. (2014). *Thriving on the front lines: A guide to strengths-based youth care work.* New York: Haworth.

Bertolino, B. (2011). Building a culture of excellence: Anatomy of a community agency that works. *Psychotherapy Networker, 35*(3), 32–39.

Bertolino, B. (2010). *Strengths-based engagement and practice: Creating effective helping relationships.* Boston: Allyn & Bacon.

Bertolino, B. (2003). *Change-oriented psychotherapy with adolescents and young adults: The next generation of respectful and effective therapeutic processes and practices.* New York: Norton.

Bertolino, B. (1999). *Therapy with troubled teenagers: Rewriting young lives in progress.* New York: Wiley.

Bertolino, B., Bargmann, S., & Miller, S. D. (2013). Manual 1: What works in therapy: A primer. The ICCE manuals of feedback informed treatment. Chicago: International Center for Clinical Excellence.

Bertolino, B., Kiener, M. S., & Patterson, R. (2009). *The therapist's notebook for strengths and solution-based therapies: Homework, handouts, and activities.* New York: Routledge/Taylor & Francis.

168 References

Bertolino, B., & O'Hanlon, B. (2002). *Collaborative, competency-based counseling and therapy.* Boston: Allyn & Bacon.

Bolin, I. (2006). *Growing up in a culture of respect: Child rearing in Highland Peru.* Austin: University of Texas Press.

Brendtro, L., du Toit, L., Bath, H., & Van Bockern, S. (2006). Developmental audits with challenging youth. *Reclaiming Children and Youth, 15*(3), 138–146.

Brown, G.S., Lambert, M.J., Jones, E.R., & Minami, T. (2005). Identifying highly effective psychotherapists in a managed care environment. *American Journal of Managed Care, 11*(8), 513–520.

Brown, L.S. (2008). *Cultural competence in trauma therapy: Beyond the flashback.* Washington, DC: American Psychological Association.

Cade, B., & O'Hanlon, W.H. (1993). *A brief guide to brief therapy.* New York: Norton.

Casey, K.J., Reid, R., Trout, A.L., Hurley, K.D., Chmelka, M.B., & Thompson, R. (2010). The transition status of youth departing residential care. *Child Youth Care Forum, 39*, 323–340.

Catalono, R.F., Berglund, M.L., Ryan, J.A.M., Lonczak, H.S., & Hawkins, J.D. (2004). Positive youth development in the United States. *The ANNALS of the American Academy of Political and Social Science, 591*, 98–124.

de Shazer, S. (1988). *Clues: Investigating solutions in brief therapy.* New York: Norton.

Duncan, B.L., Miller, S.D., & Sparks, J.A. (2004). *The heroic client: A revolutionary way to improve effectiveness through client directed, outcome-informed therapy* (Revised paperback edition). San Francisco: Jossey-Bass.

Duncan, B.L., Miller, S.D., Wampold, B.E., & Hubble, M.A. (Eds.), (2010). *The heart and soul of change: Delivering what works in therapy* (2nd ed.). Washington, DC: American Psychological Association.

Durrant, M. (1993). *Residential treatment: A cooperative, competency-based approach to therapy and program design.* New York: Norton.

Ericsson, K.A. (2009). Enhancing the development of professional performance: Implications from the study of deliberate practice. In K.A. Ericsson (Ed.), *The development of professional expertise: Toward measurement of expert performance and design of optimal learning environments* (pp. 405–431). New York: Cambridge University Press.

Ericsson, K.A., Charness, N., Feltovich, P.J., & Hoffman, R.R. (Eds.). (2006). *The Cambridge handbook of expertise and expert performance.* New York: Cambridge University Press.

Frank, J.D., & Frank, J.B. (1991). *Persuasion and healing: A comparative study of psychotherapy* (3rd ed.). Baltimore: Johns Hopkins University Press.

Freeman, J., Epston, D., & Lobovits, D. (1997). *Playful approaches to serious problems: Narrative therapy with children and their families.* New York: Norton.

Furman, B., & Ahola, T. (1992). *Solution talk: Hosting therapeutic conversations.* New York Norton.

Garcia, J.A., & Weisz, J.R. (2002). When youth mental health care stops: Therapeutic relationship problems and other reasons for ending youth outpatient treatment. *Journal of Consulting and Clinical Psychology, 70*(2), 439–443.

Gawande, A. (2007). *Better: A surgeon's notes on performance.* New York: Henry Holt and Company.

References   169

Gawande, A. (2004). The bell curve: What happens when patients find out how good their doctors really are? *New Yorker*, December 6.

Gladwell, M. (2013). *David and Goliath: Underdogs, misfits, and the art of battling giants*. New York: Little, Brown.

Gladwell, M. (2000). *The tipping point: How little things can make a big difference*. New York: Little, Brown.

Greenberg, R. P. (1999). Common factors in psychiatric drug therapy. In M. A. Hubble, B. L. Duncan, & S. D. Miller (Eds.), *The heart and soul of change: What works in therapy* (pp. 297–328). Washington, DC: American Psychological Association.

Haas, E., Hill, R. D., Lambert, M. J., & Morrell, B. (2002). Do early responders to psychotherapy maintain treatment gains? *Journal of Clinical Psychology, 58*(9), 1157–1172.

Hays, P. A. (2007). *Addressing cultural complexities in practice: Assessment diagnosis and therapy* (2nd ed.). Washington, DC: American Psychological Association.

Hill, P. L., Burrow, A. L., O'Dell, A. C., & Thornton, M. A. (2010). Classifying adolescents' conceptions of purpose in life. *Journal of Positive Psychology, 5*(6), 466–473.

Horvath, A. O., & Bedi, R. P. (2002). The alliance. In J. C. Norcross (Ed.), *Psychotherapy relationships that work: Therapist contributions and responsiveness to patient needs* (pp. 37–69). New York: Oxford University Press.

Hwang, J., & Hopkins, K. (2012). Organizational inclusion, commitment, and turnover among child welfare workers: A multilevel mediation analysis. *Administration in Social Work, 36*, 23–39.

Krueger, M. A. (1990). Promoting professional teamwork. In J. P. Anglin, C. J. Denholm, R. V. Ferguson, & A. R. Pence (Eds.), *Perspectives in professional child and youth care* (pp. 123–130). Binghamton, NY: Haworth.

Luborsky, L., Crits-Christoph, P., McLellan, T., Woody, G., Piper, W., Imber, S., & Liberman, B. (1986). Do therapists vary much in their success? Findings in four outcome studies. *American Journal of Orthopsychiatry, 56*, 501–512.

Martin, D. J., Garske, J. P., & Davis, M. K. (2000). Relationship of the therapeutic alliance with outcome and other variables: A meta-analytic review. *Journal of Consulting and Clinical Psychology, 68*(3), 438–450.

Maslow, A. H. (1943). A theory of human motivation. *Psychological Review, 50*(4), 370–396.

McBride, J. (1997). *Steven Spielberg: A biography*. New York: Simon and Schuster.

Metcalf, L. (1995). *Counseling toward solutions: A practical solution-focused program for working with students, teachers, and parents*. New York: Center for Applied Research in Education.

Miller, S. D., Duncan, B. L., & Hubble, M. A. (1997). *Escape from Babel: Toward a unifying language for psychotherapy practice*. New York: Norton.

Norcross, J. C. (Ed.). (2011). *Psychotherapy relationships that work: Evidence-based responsiveness* (2nd ed.). New York: Oxford.

O'Hanlon, B., & Bertolino, B. (1998). *Even from a broken web: Brief, respectful solution-oriented therapy for sexual abuse and trauma*. New York: John Wiley & Sons.

O'Hanlon, W. H. (1987). *Taproots: Underlying principles of Milton Erickson's therapy and hypnosis*. New York: Norton.

170   References

O'Hanlon, W.H., & Weiner-Davis, M. (2003). *In search of solutions: A new direction in psychotherapy* (2nd ed.). New York: Norton.

Orlinsky, D.E., Grawe, K., & Parks, B.K. (1994). Process and outcome in psychotherapy—noch einmal. In A.E. Bergin & S.L. Garfield (Eds.), *Handbook of psychotherapy and behavior change* (4th ed.) (pp. 270–378). New York: John Wiley & Sons.

Orlinsky, D.E., Rønnestad, M.H., & Willutzki, U. (2004). Fifty years of process-outcome research: Continuity and change. In M.J. Lambert (Ed.), *Bergin and Garfield's handbook of psychotherapy and behavior change* (5th ed.) (pp. 307–390). New York: John Wiley & Sons.

Pascale, R., Sternin, J., & Sternin, M. (2010). *The power of positive deviance: How unlikely innovators resolve the world's toughest problems.* Boston: Harvard Business Press.

Percevic, R., Lambert, M.J., & Kordy, H. (2006). What is the predictive value of responses to psychotherapy for its future course? Empirical explorations and consequences for outcome monitoring. *Psychotherapy Research, 16(3),* 364–273.

Prochaska, J.O., & DiClemente, C.C. (2005). The transtheoretical approach. In J.C. Norcross & M.R. Goldfried (Eds.), *Handbook of psychotherapy integration* (2nd ed.) (pp. 147–171). New York: Oxford University Press.

Proyouthwork America. (2011). *Youth work practice: A status report on professionalization and expert opinion about the future of the field.* Bonita Springs, FL: Proyouthwork America.

Safran, J.D., Muran, J.C., Samstag, L.W., & Stevens, C. (2002). Repairing alliance ruptures. In J.C. Norcross (Ed.), *Psychotherapy relationships that work: Therapist contributions and responsiveness to patients* (pp. 235–254). New York: Oxford University Press.

Seita, J., Mitchell, M., & Tobin, C. (1996). *In whose best interest?* Elizabethtown, PA: Continental Press.

Selekman, M. (1997). *Solution-focused therapy with children: Harnessing family strengths for systemic change.* New York: Guilford.

Seligman, M.E.P. (2011). *Flourish: A visionary new understanding of happiness and well-being.* New York: The Free Press.

Sparks, J.A., & Muro, M.L. (2009). Client-directed wraparound: The client as connector in community collaboration. *Journal of Systemic Therapies, 28(3),* 63–76.

Surowiecki, J. (2004). *The wisdom of crowds.* New York: Anchor Books.

Thomas, B. (1994). *Walt Disney: An American original.* New York: Hyperion.

Vilakazi, H. (1993). Rediscovering lost truths. *Reclaiming Children and Youth, 1(4),* 37.

Wampold, B.E. (2001). *The great psychotherapy debate: Models, methods, and findings.* Mahwah, NJ: Lawrence Erlbaum.

Wampold, B.E., & Brown, G.S. (2005). Estimating variability in outcomes attributable to therapists: A naturalistic study of outcomes in managed care. *Journal of Consulting and Clinical Psychology, 73(5),* 914–923.

Warren, J.S., Nelson, P.L., Burlingame, G.M., & Mondragon, S.A. (2012). Predicting patient deterioration in youth mental health services: Community mental health versus manager care settings. *Journal of Clinical Psychology, 68(1),* 24–40.

References 171

Whipple, J. L., Lambert, M. J., Vermeersch, D. A., Smart, D. W., Nielsen, S. L., & Hawkins, E. J. (2003). Improving the effects of psychotherapy: The use of early identification of treatment and problem-solving strategies in routine practice. *Journal of Counseling Psychology, 50*(1), 59–68.

Whitaker, R. (2010). *Anatomy of an epidemic: Magic bullets, psychiatric drugs, and the astonishing rise of mental illness in America.* New York: Crown.

White, M., & Epston, D. (1990). *Narrative means to therapeutic ends.* New York: Norton.

Wilson, M. (2009). Supporting the direct-service workforce in behavioral health programs for children and youth in New Hampshire: A report to the New Hampshire Endowment for Health. New England Network for Child, Youth and Family Services. Retrieved from www.nenetwork.org/publications/NH_Behav_Hlth_Workforce.pdf

Index

Page numbers for table are in *italics*.

abilities 10–11, 74, 102, 105, 120–2
accommodation 14, 66
accomplishments 11, 155–6
accountability 30, 102–5, 151
ACE (Active Client Engagement) 43
achievement 11, 56
acknowledgment: communicating
    44–5; in crisis situations 134–5;
    of perspective differences 72–3;
    of problems 118; using 102–3; of
    viewpoints 81
actions 92, 110–12, 123
action-talk 57–8, 61, 66, 77, 80, 111,
    158
Active Client Engagement (ACE) 43
ADDRESSING acronym 15
agencies 34
agreement 14
alliances 11–12; building 29;
    measurement 62–3, 80, 107;
    therapeutic 14–15, 41
Appelstein, C. 131
assessments 38, 40–3, 49–50, 55, 96
assumptions 7, 12, 38–9, 64, 72, 83
attitudes 8, 19, 40
attribution 151–3

basic needs 17
benefits of services 17, 62–3, 148
Bertolino, B.: *Thriving on the Front
    Lines: A Guide to Strengths-Based
    Youth Care Work* 12, 63, 68–9, 79,
    93, 110, 112
*Better: A Surgeon's Notes on
    Performance* (Gawande) 8
biological intervention 17
blame 100, 151

broken window theory 34
Brown, L. S. 15–16
Burlingame, G. M. 63

caregivers 56–7, 154–6
case conferences *see* meetings
CCH (Cincinnati Children's Hospital)
    124–5
CF (cystic fibrosis) 124–5
change: catalysts of 18–20;
    expectancy of 18–19; identifying
    145; language of 22–30; and level
    programs 64; meaningful 17–18;
    measuring 63, 148–9; relevance of
    159–61; tracking 155–6; of views
    98–9; *see also* actions; interactions
Cincinnati Children's Hospital (CCH)
    124–5
clarity, seeking 80–4
clients 12–13, 39–40
collaboration: goals 56–7; and
    information gathering 49–55;
    language and 22–3, 26; with youth
    14, 21
collaboration key 42
collecting evidence 155–6, *157*, *158*
Collective Goal Groups *129*
communication 22, 32, 43
community meetings 126–31
competency 120–2
conferences *see* meetings
congruence 43–4
conjecture 106–7
consultation 134
control 151
conversations: about service benefits
    78–9, 84; for accountability 105;

174 *Index*

for improvement 147; to open closed-down statements 45–6; pathology-based 71–2; personal philosophy 30–2; strengths-based 23–5, *24–5*, 28–9, 107–8, 127–8; *see also* language
coping-sequence questions 122–3
coping styles 94–5
costs of being average 125
counterexamples 104–5
creating possibilities 48–9
credit sharing 153–4
crises: de-escalating 134–8; management 132–4; on-call systems 138–43; prevention 125–6, 131–2
cross-mirroring 135
cultural influences 15–17
curiosity 106–7, 111
cystic fibrosis (CF) 124–5

Darwin, C. 69
de-escalation methods 134–9
defensiveness 32
deficits 7, 17, 22
depatterning 112–15
deterioration 96–7, 145–6
development 17–18, 93, 161
Diagnostic and Statistical Manual of Mental Disorders (DSM) 49
Disneyland *see* Walt Disney Company
distraction 137–8
dream method 58–9
dropping out 97, 145
DSM (*Diagnostic and Statistical Manual of Mental Disorders*) 49
Durrant, M. 6, 20, 64

effect 93, 96–8
effectiveness 17–18
80/20 rule 55, 160–1
empathy 43–4
end points 118–20
engagement 11
environments of involvement 14
Erickson, M. 111
evaluations 35, 38
evidence collecting 155–6, *157*, *158*
exceptions: and accountability 102–5; and competency 120–2; in crisis situations 134, 142–3; seeking 51–5, 80–4, 99–100
expectancy-talk 107–8
expectations 18–20

experience: internal 103–4; interpreting 32; for problem solving 116–18; of residential facility 37–8; talking about 41–2; of team members 69; and turnover rate 6
external resources 13

FastPass 60
family time-outs 56
feedback 11–12, 14, 62
fit 93–6
forecasting effect 38
Freireich, E. 40
frustration 87, 89–90
future 148, 159
future pull 107–10

Galton, F. 69
Gawande, A. 40, 124–5; *Better: A Surgeon's Notes on Performance* 8
genuineness 43–4
goals 17; collaborative 56–7; group 128–31, *129*, *130*; measurement of 160; problems into 108
good fit 14
group meetings 126–31
growth 13, 17–18, 161
guidelines 41

handoffs 134
Hays, P. A. 15
homelessness 55–6
hope 18–20, 40
hot buttons 132
humor, using 138–9
hyperarousal 132

iatrogenic injury 22
illusion of alternatives 136–7
impossibility 100
improvement 96–7, 145
Individual Goal Groups *130*
information 28, 38, 40–53, 133
initial contacts 36–9
intake assessment 41, 49–55
interactions 43, 81, 92, 110–12
interpersonal functioning 11
interventions: crisis prevention 131; fit of 93–6; rationale for 17
interviews 41
invalidation 100

key tasks 13–14, 15, 16, 18, 19–20

Index   175

labels 29, 104
language: for change 22–30, 102; of engagement 43–4; perspective and 72–3; in petition for higher levels 66; philosophy and 30–2, 35; possibility-laced 107; vocabularies 23–4, *24*; *see also* conversations
Letter of Evidence *157*
level systems 63–6, *65*
linking 158–9
listening space 41–3

Maslow, A. H. 12
maturation 13
meaning 11
measurements 62–3, 148, 160
medications 105
meetings: group 126–31; productivity of 78–84; and service planning 76–8; sharing results of 84; shift change 86–91; team 70–6, 125–6
memories 155
mental health professionals 17
Metcalf, L. 30
miracle question 58
mirroring 135
momentum 156–9
Mondragon, S. A. 63
moving walkway 107–8
multiple-choice options 117

negativity 70–3
Nelson, P. L. 63
New Yorker magazine 124
no improvement 96–7, 145
nonaccountability 100, 103
nonverbal behavior 133

O'Hanlon, W. H. 99
on-call systems 139–43
open door policy 42
opinion, diversity of 69
options 136–7
orienting 95
outcomes 11–12, 17–18; effect of 96–8; goals and 160–1; measuring 62–3, 148
out-of-home placements 3–4

paraphrasing 44–6
pathology 6–7, 10, 17, 22–30
patterns: of behavior 92; depatterning 112–15; repatterning 115–23

PCD (post-crisis debriefings) 142
perceptual statements 47
perspectives 6, 40
personal philosophy 7–9, 38–9, 115; and language 30–2; and negativity 71–2
pessimism 19, 40
positive deviance 33–5
Positive Psychology 93
positive regard 43–4
Positive Youth Development (PYD) 93
possibilities 7–8, 21–2, 48–9
possibility-accountability 30
possibility-talk 45–9
post-crisis debriefings (PCD) 142
presupposition 108–9, 116, 135, 149
primary competency 12–19
private placements 55–6
problems: changing patterns of 112–15; end points of 118–20; goals from 108; stories about 99–100
problem-talk 29–31, *30*, 71–2, 118
process measurement 11–12
progress: and goals 159; lack of 145–6; monitoring 80, 97, 148; negative conversations and 71; reporting at shift change 86; signposts 60–4
promotions 64
protective factors 13
protocols 132
psychotherapy research 39–40
PYD (Positive Youth Development) 93

questions: change 66, 145–6, 148–9, 151–2, 157, 159–64; coping-sequence 122–3; credit sharing 153–4; crisis prevention 125–6; end points identification 118; exception-oriented 51–5, 101–2, 148–9; goals 56–7, 128; initial contact 43, 50–5; for intervention methods 94; miracle 58; orienting 95; for pattern finding 111; personal philosophy 7–8; post-crisis debriefings 142; for preferred future 109–10; service plan 76–7; at shift changes 86–7; signposts 61; for solutions finding 116; speculations 150; strengths-based 49–55; time machine 59; vocabulary 23; "why" 122; for YCWs 3

rap sheets 38
real-time feedback 11–12, 14, 17

176 *Index*

Redford, R. 70
reflection 30–2, 143
relational styles 43
relationships: building 72–3; and
coping skills 131; therapeutic
14–15; of youth and residential
workers 9–12, 41–3, 145–7
repatterning 112, 115–23
residential facilities 4
residential programs 32–5
residential workers: attitudes of 40;
characteristics of 74; duties of 4–5;
goals of 82; guidelines for 68–70;
and interaction with youth 43;
longevity issues 5–6; negativity and
70–3; on-call 139–43; perspective
of 6–7, 79–80; philosophy of 7–9;
profile 3–4; responsibilities of 67–8;
shift-change frustration of 87,
89–90; strength list 73; training for
92; weekly success chart 75
residential youth care workers
(RYCWs) *see* residential workers
resilience factors 13
respect 15–16
rituals 164
Road Runner 46
role-plays 132
RYCWs (residential youth care
workers) *see* residential workers

safety concerns 133
Save the Children Campaign 33
saving face option 137
screening 49–50
self-care 165
self-knowledge 132
service planning 76–8
services: benefits of 7; effects of
18–20; purpose of 55–6
setbacks 64
sharing 84
Shelter, The 2
shelter shuffle 16, 37, 39
shift changes 86–91, *88*
signposts 60–2
simplicity 85
site effects 35
sleep shifts 5
social role functioning 11, 145–7
social skills 81
solution-talk 30, *30*, 72, 118
speaking up 74–6
speculation 29, 150–2

Spielberg, S. 100
staff infections (negative
conversations) 71
staffings *see* meetings
Sternin, J. and M. 33–4
stories: change 152–3; developing
154–6; initial interview 41–3;
negative 30–2; problematic 99–100;
transition 162–4
strengths 131–2
strengths-based: crisis management
142; conversational style 28–9;
culture 32; defined 10–11;
principles 12–20; programs 7;
vocabularies 23, *24*
stress 132
subjective interpretations 17
successes 34–5, 70–1, 93
summarizing 44–6
support 134

tantrums 113
tasks 13–14, 15, 16, 18, 19–20
team approach 67–9
teams 34, 85–6
therapeutic alliance 11, 14–15, 41
Thomas, K. S. 70
*Thriving on the Front Lines: A Guide
to Strengths-Based Youth Care
Work* (Bertolino) 12, 63, 68–9, 79,
93, 110, 112
time limits 85
time machine, the 59
time-outs 56
tools, measurement 63
traditional/deficit-driven programs 7
training 92
transitions 161–4
treatment savvy 37
troubleshooting in advance 131

validation 44–5; in crisis situations
134; of problems 118
video talk 58
views 92, 98–102, 105–7
vision 21–2, 32–4, 55–6, 107–10, 159
visualizing 59–60
vocabularies 22–3, *24*

Walt Disney Company 21–2, 32–5,
60–1
Warren, J. S. 63
Weekly Evidence Log *158*
Weiner-Davis, M. 99

Index 177

well-being 11, 14, 17–18, 62, 93
"why" questions 122–3
wisdom of crowds, the 69
working alliance 14, 41
wraparound process 85–6

YIN (Youth In Need) 1–2
youth 77; abilities of 11; alliances
with 14–15, 29; and alternative
viewpoints 105–7; as consultants
164; contributors to service success
12–14; and crisis prevention 132;
culture of 15–16; decision making
with 77–8; descriptions of 100;
empowering 17–18; engaging
44; historical information about
38–40; and problem alignment
94–8; and problem solving 8; and
shift changes 90–1; stories about
99–100; transitions 161–4; and
wraparound plan 85–6
Youth and Family Services (YFS) 1, 3
youth care workers (YCWs) 3
Youth In Need (YIN) 1–2